Or.	pg. 830	Bapt. I
Gifts	pg. 832	Bapt. II
Pref.	1 54	HS I
Comm.	pg. 83$\frac{\text{or } 29}{3}$	Bapt. II

52   155 or 148

RITE OF BAPTISM
FOR CHILDREN

THE ROMAN RITUAL

Revised by the Second Vatican Ecumenical Council
and Published by Authority of Pope Paul VI

RITE OF BAPTISM
FOR CHILDREN

English Translation Approved by
the National Conference of Catholic Bishops
and Confirmed by the Apostolic See

THE LITURGICAL PRESS
Collegeville, Minnesota

www.litpress.org

Concordat cum originali:

Monsignor James P. Moroney
Executive Director
USCCB Secretariat for the Liturgy

Cover design by Frank Kacmarcik, Obl.S.B.

RITE OF BAPTISM
FOR CHILDREN

SACRED CONGREGATION FOR DIVINE WORSHIP

Prot. no. R 23/969

DECREE

The Second Vatican Council decreed that the rite of baptism for children in the Roman Ritual should be revised in order that:

a) the rite might be better adapted to the actual condition of children;

b) the role and responsibilities of parents and godparents might be more clearly expressed;

c) suitable adaptations might be made for the baptism of a large number of people;

d) suitable adaptations might likewise be made for baptism administered by catechists in mission areas or by others in circumstances when the ordinary minister is unavailable;

e) a rite might be provided for use when a child has already been baptized according to the shorter rite, to mark the fact that he has already been received into the Church (Constitution on the Sacred Liturgy, nos. 67–69).

This revision has been carried out by the Consilium for the Implementation of the Constitution on the Sacred Liturgy. By his apostolic authority Pope Paul VI has approved this new rite of baptism for children and directs that it should be published to replace the rite given in the Roman Ritual.

Therefore this Sacred Congregation, acting on the express mandate of the Pope, promulgates this rite to be effective September 8, 1969.

Anything to the contrary notwithstanding.

From the Congregation for Divine Worship, May 15, 1969, Feast of the Ascension.

Benno Card. Gut
Prefect

A. Bugnini
Secretary

SACRED CONGREGATION
FOR DIVINE WORSHIP

Prot. no. 1887/69

THE UNITED STATES OF AMERICA

At the request of His Excellency, John Cardinal Dearden, Archbishop of Detroit and President of the Conference of Bishops of the United States of America, in a letter of 26 November 1969, the following are approved and confirmed by the authority of the faculty granted to this Sacred Congregation by the Supreme Pontiff Paul VI:

The English text for the Order of the Baptism of Children, the Order for the Celebration of Marrige and the Litany the of Saints (with emandations as noted), arranged by the mixed Commission for English-speaking regions and attached to this Decree; [. . .]

In published editions of these texts, however, mention must be made of the confirmation granted by the Apostolic See.

Two copies of each of these above texts, when published, must be transmitted to this Sacred Congregation.

All things to the contrary notwithstanding.

Given at the Sacred Congregation for Divine Worship, 5 January 1970.

Benno Card. Gut
Prefect

A. Bugnini
Secretary

CONTENTS

CHRISTIAN INITIATION
GENERAL INTRODUCTION

1. In the sacraments of Christian initiation we are freed from the power of darkness and joined to Christ's death, burial, and resurrection. We receive the Spirit of filial adoption and are part of the entire people of God in the celebration of the memorial of the Lord's death and resurrection.[1]

2. Baptism incorporates us into Christ and forms us into God's people. This first sacrament pardons all our sins, rescues us from the power of darkness, and brings us to the the dignity of adopted children,[2] a new creation through water and the Holy Spirit. Hence we are called and are indeed the children of God.[3]

By signing us with the gift of the Spirit, confirmation makes us more completely the image of the Lord and fills us with the Holy Spirit, so that we may bear witness to him before all the world and work to bring the Body of Christ to its fullness as soon as possible.[4]

Finally, coming to the table of the eucharist, we eat the flesh and drink the blood of the Son of Man so that we may have eternal life[5] and show forth the unity of God's people. By offering ourselves with Christ, we share in the universal sacrifice, that is, the entire community of the redeemed offered to God by their High Priest,[6] and we pray for a greater outpouring of the Holy Spirit, so that the whole human race may be brought into the unity of God's family.[7]

Thus the three sacraments of Christian initiation closely combine to bring us, the faithful of Christ, to his full stature and to enable us to carry out the mission of the entire people of God in the Church and in the world.[8]

DIGNITY OF BAPTISM

3. Baptism, the door to life and to the kingdom of God, is the first sacrament of the New Law, which Christ offered to all, that they might

---

[1] See Vatican Council II, Decree on the Church's Missionary Activity *Ad gentes,* no. 14.

[2] Colossians 1:13; Romans 8:15; Galatians 4:5. See also Council of Trent, sess. 6, *Decr. de iustificatione* cap. 4: Denz.-Schön. 1524.

[3] See 1 John 3:1.

[4] See Vatican Council II, Decree on the Church's Missionary Activity *Ad gentes,* no. 36.

[5] See John 6:55.

[6] See Augustine, *De civitate Dei,* 10,6: PL 41, 284. Vatican Council II, Dogmatic Constitution on the Church *Lumen gentium,* no. 11; Decree on the Ministry and Life of Priests, *Presbyterorum Ordinis,* no. 2.

[7] See Vatican Council II, Dogmatic Constitution on the Church, *Lumen gentium,* no. 28.

[8] See ibid., no. 31.

have eternal life.[9] He later entrusted this sacrament and the Gospel to his Church, when he told his apostles: "Go, make disciples of all nations, and baptize them in the name of the Father, and of the Son, and of the Holy Spirit."[10] Baptism is therefore, above all, the sacrament of that faith by which, enlightened by the grace of the Holy Spirit, we respond to the Gospel of Christ. That is why the Church believes that it is its most basic and necessary duty to inspire all, catechumens, parents of children still to be baptized, and godparents, to that true and living faith by which they hold fast to Christ and enter into or confirm their commitment to the New Covenant. In order to enliven such faith, the Church prescribes the pastoral instruction of catechumens, the preparation of the children's parents, the celebration of God's word, and the profession of faith at the celebration of baptism.

4. Further, baptism is the sacrament by which its recipients are incorporated into the Church and are built up together in the Spirit into a house where God lives,[11] into a holy nation and a royal priesthood.[12] Baptism is a sacramental bond of unity linking all who have been signed by it.[13] Because of that unchangeable effect (given expression in the Latin liturgy by the anointing of the baptized person with chrism in the presence of God's people), the rite of baptism is held in highest honor by all Christians. Once it has been validly celebrated, even if by Christians with whom we are not in full communion, it may never lawfully be repeated.

5. Baptism, the cleansing with water by the power of the living word,[14] washes away every stain of sin, original and personal, makes us sharers in God's own life[15] and his adopted children.[16] As proclaimed in the prayers for the blessing of the water, baptism is a cleansing water of rebirth[17] that makes us God's children born from on high. The blessed Trinity is invoked over those who are to be baptized, so that all who are signed in this name are consecrated to the Trinity and enter into communion with the Father, the Son, and the Holy Spirit. They are prepared for this high dignity and led to it by the scriptural readings, the prayer of the community, and their own profession of belief in the Father, the Son, and the Holy Spirit.

[9] See John 3:5.
[10] Matthew 28:19.
[11] See Ephesians 2:22.
[12] See 1 Peter 2:9.
[13] See Vatican Council II, Decree on Ecumenism *Unitatis redintegratio,* no. 22.
[14] See Ephesians 5:26.
[15] See 2 Peter 1:4.
[16] See Romans 8:15; Galatians 4:5.
[17] See Titus 3:5.

6. Far superior to the purifications of the Old Law, baptism produces these effects by the power of the mystery of the Lord's passion and resurrection. Those who are baptized are united to Christ in a death like his;[18] buried with him in death, they are given life again with him, and with him they rise again.[19] For baptism recalls and makes present the paschal mystery itself, because in baptism we pass from the death of sin into life. The celebration of baptism should therefore reflect the joy of the resurrection, especially when the celebration takes place during the Easter Vigil or on a Sunday.

OFFICES AND MINISTRIES OF BAPTISM

7. The preparation for baptism and Christian instruction are both a vital concern of God's people, the Church, which hands on and nourishes the faith received from the apostles. Through the ministry of the Church, adults are called to the Gospel by the Holy Spirit and infants are baptized in the faith of the Church and brought up in that faith. Therefore it is most important that catechists and other laypersons should work with priests and deacons in the preparation for baptism. In the actual celebration, the people of God (represented not only by the parents, godparents, and relatives, but also, as far as possible, by friends, neighbors, and some members of the local Church) should take an active part. Thus they will show their common faith and the shared joy with which the newly baptized are received into the community of the Church.

8. It is a very ancient custom of the Church that adults are not admitted to baptism without godparents, members of the Christian community who will assist the candidates at least in the final preparation for baptism and after baptism will help them persevere in the faith and in their lives as Christians. In the baptism of children, as well, godparents are to be present in order to represent both the expanded spiritual family of the one to be baptized and the role of the Church as a mother. As occasion offers, godparents help the parents so that children will come to profess the faith and live up to it.

9. At least in the later rites of the catechumenate and in the actual celebration of baptism, the part of the godparents is to testify to the faith of the adult candidates or, together with the parents, to profess the Church's faith, in which the children are baptized.

10. Therefore godparents, chosen by the catechumens or by the families of children to be baptized, must, in the judgment of the pastor, be qualified to carry out the proper liturgical functions mentioned in no. 9.

[18] See Romans 6:4-5.
[19] See Ephesians 2:5-6.

1) Godparents are persons, other than the parents of candidates, who are designated by the candidates themselves or by a candidate's parents or whoever stands in place of parents, or, in the absence of these, by the pastor or the minister of baptism. Each candidate may have either a godmother or a godfather or both a godmother and a godfather.

2) Those designated must have the capability and intention of carrying out the responsibility of a godparent and be mature enough to do so. A person sixteen years of age is presumed to have the requisite maturity, but the diocesan bishop may have stipulated another age or the pastor or the minister may decide that there is a legitimate reason for allowing an exception.

3) Those designated as godparents must have received the three sacraments of initiation, baptism, confirmation, and eucharist, and be living a life consistent with faith and with the responsibility of a godparent.

4) Those designated as godparents must also be members of the Catholic Church and be canonically free to carry out this office. At the request of parents, a baptized and believing Christian not belonging to the Catholic Church may act as a Christian witness along with a Catholic godparent.[20] In the case of separated Eastern Christians with whom we do not have full communion the special discipline for the Eastern Churches is to be respected.

11. The ordinary ministers of baptism are bishops, priests, and deacons.

1) In every celebration of this sacrament they should be mindful that they act in the Church in the name of Christ and by the power of the Holy Spirit.

2) They should therefore be diligent in the ministry of the word of God and in the manner of celebrating the sacrament. They must avoid any action that the faithful could rightly regard as favoritism.[21]

3) Except in a case of necessity, these ministers are not to confer baptism outside their own territory, even on their own subjects, without the requisite permission.

12. Bishops are the chief stewards of the mysteries of God and leaders of the entire liturgical life in the Church committed to them.[22] This is why they direct the conferring of baptism, which brings to the recipient a share in the kingly priesthood of Christ.[23] Therefore bishops

---

[20] See *Codex Iuris Canonici,* can. 873 and 874, §§1 and 2.

[21] See Vatican Council II, Constitution on the Liturgy, *Sacrosanctum Concilium,* art. 32; Pastoral Constitution on the Church in the Modern World *Gaudium et spes,* no. 29.

[22] See Vatican Council II, Decree on the Pastoral Office of Bishops *Christus Dominus,* no. 15.

[23] See Vatican Council II, Dogmatic Constitution on the Church *Lumen gentium,* no. 26.

should personally celebrate baptism, especially at the Easter Vigil. They should have a particular concern for the preparation and baptism of adults.

13. It is the duty of pastors to assist the bishop in the instruction and baptism of the adults entrusted to their care, unless the bishop makes other provisions. Pastors, with the assistance of catechists or other qualified laypersons, have the duty of preparing the parents and godparents of children through appropriate pastoral guidance and of baptizing the children.

14. Other priests and deacons, since they are co-workers in the ministry of bishops and pastors, also prepare candidates for baptism and, by the invitation or consent of the bishop or pastor, celebrate the sacrament.

15. The celebrant of baptism may be assisted by other priests and deacons and also by laypersons in those parts that pertain to them, especially if there are a large number to be baptized. Provision for this is made in various parts of the rituals for adults and for children.

16. In imminent danger of death and especially at the moment of death, when no priest or deacon is available, any member of the faithful, indeed anyone with the right intention, may and sometimes must administer baptism. In a case simply of danger of death the sacrament should be administered, if possible, by a member of the faithful according to one of the shorter rites provided for this situation.[24] Even in this case a small community should be formed to assist at the rite or, if possible, at least one or two witnesses should be present.

17. Since they belong to the priestly people, all laypersons, especially parents and, by reason of their work, catechists, midwives, family or social workers or nurses of the sick, as well as physicians and surgeons, should be thoroughly aware, according to their capacities, of the proper method of baptizing in case of emergency. They should be taught by pastors, deacons, and catechists. Bishops should provide appropriate means within their diocese for such instruction.

REQUIREMENTS FOR THE CELEBRATION OF BAPTISM

18. The water used in baptism should be true water and, both for the sake of authentic sacramental symbolism and for hygienic reasons, should be pure and clean.

19. The baptismal font, or the vessel in which on occasion the water is prepared for celebration of the sacrament in the sanctuary, should be spotlessly clean and of pleasing design.

---

[24] See *Rite of Christian Initiation of Adults,* nos. 375–399; *Rite of Baptism for Children,* nos. 157–164.

20. If the climate requires, provision should be made for the water to be heated beforehand.

21. Except in case of necessity, a priest or deacon is to use only water that has been blessed for the rite. The water blessed at the Easter Vigil should, if possible, be kept and used throughout the Easter season to signify more clearly the relationship between the sacrament of baptism and the paschal mystery. Outside the Easter season, it is desirable that the water be blessed for each occasion, in order that the words of blessing may explicitly express the mystery of salvation that the Church remembers and proclaims. If the baptistery is supplied with running water, the blessing is given as the water flows.

22. As the rite for baptizing, either immersion, which is more suitable as a symbol of participation in the death and resurrection of Christ, or pouring may lawfully be used.

23. The words for conferring baptism in the Latin Church are:
I BAPTIZE YOU IN THE NAME OF THE FATHER, AND OF THE SON, AND OF THE HOLY SPIRIT.

24. For celebrating the liturgy of the word of God a suitable place should be provided in the baptistery or in the church.

25. The baptistery or the area where the baptismal font is located should be reserved for the sacrament of baptism and should be worthy to serve as the place where Christians are reborn in water and the Holy Spirit. The baptistery may be situated in a chapel either inside or outside the church or in some other part of the church easily seen by the faithful; it should be large enough to accommodate a good number of people. After the Easter season, the Easter candle should be kept reverently in the baptistery, in such a way that it can be lighted for the celebration of baptism and so that from it the candles for the newly baptized can easily be lighted.

26. In the celebration the parts of the rite that are to be celebrated outside the baptistery should be carried out in different areas of the church that most conveniently suit the size of the congregation and the several parts of the baptismal liturgy. When the baptistery cannot accommodate all the catechumens and the congregation, the parts of the rite that are customarily celebrated inside the baptistery may be transferred to some other suitable area of the church.

27. As far as possible, all recently born babies should be baptized at a common celebration on the same day. Except for a good reason, baptism should not be celebrated more than once on the same day in the same church.

28. Further details concerning the time for baptism of adults and of children will be found in the respective rituals. But at all times the celebration of the sacrament should have a markedly paschal character.

29. Pastors must carefully and without delay record in the baptismal register the names of those baptized, of the minister, parents, and godparents, as well as the place and date of baptism.

ADAPTATIONS BY THE CONFERENCES OF BISHOPS

30. According to the Constitution on the Liturgy (art. 63, b), it is within the competence of the conferences of bishops to compose for their local rituals a section corresponding to this one in the Roman Ritual, adapted to the needs of their respective regions. After it has been reviewed by the Apostolic See, it may be used in the regions for which it was prepared.

In this connection, it is the responsibility of each conference of bishops:

1) to decide on the adaptations mentioned in the Constitution on the Liturgy (art. 39);

2) carefully and prudently to weigh what elements of a people's distinctive traditions and culture may suitably be admitted into divine worship and so to propose to the Apostolic See other adaptations considered useful or necessary that will be introduced with its consent;

3) to retain distinctive elements of any existing local rituals, as long as they conform to the Constitution on the Liturgy and correspond to contemporary needs, or to modify these elements;

4) to prepare translations of the texts that genuinely reflect the characteristics of various languages and cultures and to add, whenever helpful, music suitable for singing;

5) to adapt and augment the Introductions contained in the Roman Ritual, so that the ministers may fully understand the meaning of the rites and carry them out effectively;

6) to arrange the material in the various editions of the liturgical books prepared under the guidance of the conference of bishops, so that these books may better suit pastoral use.

31. Taking into consideration especially the norms in the Constitution on the Liturgy (art. 37–40, 65), the conferences of bishops in mission countries have the responsibility of judging whether the elements of initiation in use among some peoples can be adapted for the rite of Christian baptism and of deciding whether such elements are to be incorporated into the rite.

32. When the Roman Ritual for baptism provides several optional formularies, local rituals may add other formularies of the same kind.

33. The celebration of baptism is greatly enhanced by the use of song, which stimulates in the participants a sense of unity, fosters their praying together, and expresses the joy of Easter that should permeate

the whole rite. The conference of bishops should therefore encourage and help specialists in music to compose settings for those liturgical texts particularly suited to congregational singing.

ADAPTATIONS BY THE MINISTER OF BAPTISM

34. Taking into account existing circumstances and other needs, as well as the wishes of the faithful, the minister should make full use of the various options allowed in the rite.

35. In addition to the adaptations that are provided in the Roman Ritual for the dialogue and blessings, the minister may make other adaptations for special circumstances. These adaptations will be indicated more fully in the Introductions to the rites of baptism for adults and for children.

BAPTISM OF CHILDREN

INTRODUCTION

I. IMPORTANCE OF BAPTIZING CHILDREN

1. The term "children" or "infants" refers to those who have not yet reached the age of discernment and therefore cannot profess personal faith.

2. From the earliest times, the Church, to which the mission of preaching the Gospel and of baptizing was entrusted, has baptized not only adults but children as well. Our Lord said: "Unless a man is reborn in water and the Holy Spirit, he cannot enter the kingdom of God."[1] The Church has always understood these words to mean that children should not be deprived of baptism, because they are baptized in the faith of the Church, a faith proclaimed for them by their parents and godparents, who represent both the local Church and the whole society of saints and believers: "The whole Church is the mother of all and the mother of each."[2]

3. To fulfill the true meaning of the sacrament, children must later be formed in the faith in which they have been baptized. The foundation of this formation will be the sacrament itself that they have already received. Christian formation, which is their due, seeks to lead them gradually to learn God's plan in Christ, so that they may ultimately accept for themselves the faith in which they have been baptized.

II. MINISTRIES AND ROLES IN THE CELEBRATION OF BAPTISM

4. The people of God, that is, the Church, made present by the local community, has an important part to play in the baptism of both children and adults.

Before and after the celebration of the sacrament, the child has a right to the love and help of the community. During the rite, in addition to the ways of congregational participation mentioned in the General Introduction to Christian Initiation no. 7, the community exercises its duty when it expresses its assent together with the celebrant after the profession of faith by the parents and godparents. In this way it is clear that the faith in which the children are baptized is not the private possession of the individual family, but the common treasure of the whole Church of Christ.

[1] John 3:5.
[2] Saint Augustine, Epistle 98, 5: PL 33, 362.

5. Because of the natural relationships, parents have a ministry and a responsibility in the baptism of infants more important than those of the godparents.

1) Before the celebration of the sacrament, it is of great importance that parents, moved by their own faith or with the help of friends or other members of the community, should prepare to take part in the rite with understanding. They should be provided with suitable means such as books, letters addressed to them, and catechisms designed for families. The pastor should make it his duty to visit them or see that they are visited; he should try to gather a group of families together and prepare them for the coming celebration by pastoral counsel and common prayer.

2) It is very important that the parents be present at the celebration in which their child is reborn in water and the Holy Spirit.

3) In the celebration of baptism, the father and mother have special parts to play. They listen to the words addressed to them by the celebrant, they join in prayer along with the congregation, and they exercise a genuine ministry when:

a) they publicly ask that the child be baptized;

b) they sign their child with the sign of the cross after the celebrant;

c) they renounce Satan and recite the profession of faith;

d) they (and especially the mother) carry the child to the font;

e) they hold the lighted candle;

f) they are blessed with the prayers formulated specifically for mothers and fathers.

4) A parent unable to make the profession of faith (for example, not being a Catholic) may keep silent. Such a parent, when making the request for the child's baptism is asked only to make arrangements or at least to give permission for the child's instruction in the faith of its baptism.

5) After baptism it is the responsibility of the parents, in their gratitude to God and in fidelity to the duty they have undertaken, to assist the child to know God, whose adopted child it has become, to prepare the child to receive confirmation and participate in the holy eucharist. In this duty they are again to be helped by the pastor by suitable means.

6. Each child may have a godfather *(patrinus)* and a godmother *(matrina);* the word "godparents" is used in the rite to describe both.

7. In addition to what is said about the ordinary minister of baptism in the General Introduction to Christian Initiation nos. 11–15, the following should be noted:

1) It is the duty of the priest to prepare families for the baptism of their children and to help them in the task of Christian formation that they have undertaken. It is the duty of the bishop to coordinate such pastoral efforts in the diocese, with the help also of deacons and lay people.

2) It is also the duty of the priest to arrange that baptism is always celebrated with proper dignity and, as far as possible, adapted to the circumstances and wishes of the families concerned. All who perform the rite of baptism should do so with exactness and reverence; they must also try to be understanding and friendly to all.

III. TIME AND PLACE FOR THE BAPTISM OF CHILDREN

8. As for the time of baptism, the first consideration is the welfare of the child, that it may not be deprived of the benefit of the sacrament; then the health of the mother must be considered, so that, if at all possible, she too may be present. Then, as long as they do not interfere with the greater good of the child, there are pastoral considerations, such as allowing sufficient time to prepare the parents and to plan the actual celebration in order to bring out its true character effectively.

Accordingly:

1) If the child is in danger of death, it is to be baptized without delay; this is permitted even when the parents are opposed and even when the infant is the child of non-Catholic parents. The baptism is conferred in the manner laid down in no. 21.

2) In other cases the parents, or at least one of them or whoever stands in the place of the parents, must consent to the baptism of the infant. So that proper preparation may be made for the celebration of the sacrament, as soon as possible, if need be even before the child is born, the parents should be in touch with the pastor concerning the baptism.

3) An infant should be baptized within the first weeks after birth. In the complete absence of any well-founded hope that the infant will be brought up in the Catholic religion, the baptism is to be delayed, in conformity with the provisions of particular law (see no. 25), and the parents are to be informed of the reasons.

4) In the absence of the conditions laid down in nos. 2 and 3, it is for the pastor, keeping in mind whatever regulations have been laid down by the conference of bishops, to determine the time for the baptism of infants.

9. To bring out the paschal character of baptism, it is recommended that the sacrament be celebrated during the Easter Vigil or on Sunday, when the Church commemorates the Lord's resurrection. On Sunday,

baptism may be celebrated even during Mass, so that the entire community may be present and the relationship between baptism and eucharist may be clearly seen; but this should not be done too often. Regulations for the celebration of baptism during the Easter Vigil or at Mass on Sunday will be set out later.

10. So that baptism may clearly appear as the sacrament of the Church's faith and of incorporation into the people of God, it should normally be celebrated in the parish church, which must have a baptismal font.

11. After consulting the local pastor, the local Ordinary may permit or direct that a baptismal font be placed in another church or oratory within the parish boundaries. In these places, too, the right to celebrate baptism belongs ordinarily to the pastor.

However, distance or other circumstances may make it seriously inconvenient for the candidate to go or be brought to the usual place for baptism. In such a case, the sacrament may and should be conferred in another, more accessible church or oratory or even in some other suitable place. The provisions laid down here, nos. 8–9 and 15–22, on the time and the structure of the celebration are to be followed.

12. Outside a case of necessity, baptism is not to be celebrated in private homes, unless the local Ordinary has, for a serious reason, granted permission.

13. Unless the bishop decides otherwise (see no. 11), baptism should not be celebrated in hospitals, except in cases of emergency or for some other compelling pastoral reason. But care should always be taken that the parish priest is notified and that the parents are suitably prepared beforehand.

14. While the liturgy of the word is being celebrated, it is desirable that children should be taken to some other place. But provision must be made for the mothers or godmothers to attend the liturgy of the word; the children should therefore be entrusted to the care of other women.

IV. Structure of the Rite of Baptizing Children

A. Order of Baptism Celebrated by the Ordinary Minister

15. Baptism, whether for one child, or for several, or even for a larger number, should be celebrated by the ordinary minister and with the full rite when there is no immediate danger of death.

16. The rite begins with the reception of the children. This is to indicate the desire of the parents and godparents, as well as the inten-

tion of the Church, concerning the celebration of the sacrament of baptism. These purposes are expressed in action when the parents and the celebrant trace the sign of the cross on the foreheads of the children.

17. Then the liturgy of the word is directed toward stirring up the faith of the parents, godparents, and congregation and toward praying in common for the fruits of baptism before the sacrament itself. This part of the celebration consists of the reading of one or more passages from holy Scripture; a homily, followed by a period of silence; the general intercessions, with its concluding prayer, drawn up in the style of an exorcism, to introduce either the anointing with the oil of catechumens or the laying on of hands.

18. In the celebration of the sacrament:

1) The immediate preparation consists of:

a) the solemn prayer of the celebrant, which, by invoking God and recalling his plan of salvation, blesses the water of baptism or makes reference to its earlier blessing;

b) the renunciation of Satan on the part of parents and godparents and their profession of faith, to which is added the assent of the celebrant and the community; and the final interrogation of the parents and godparents.

2) The sacrament itself consists of the washing in water by way of immersion or infusion, depending on local custom, and the invocation of the blessed Trinity.

3) The completion of the sacrament consists, first, of the anointing with chrism, which signifies the royal priesthood of the baptized and enrollment into the company of the people of God; then of the ceremonies of the white garment, lighted candle, and *ephphetha* rite (the last of which is optional).

19. Before the altar to prefigure the future sharing in the eucharist, the celebrant introduces and all recite the Lord's Prayer, in which God's children pray to their Father in heaven. Finally, a prayer of blessing is said over the mothers, fathers, and all present, to ask the outpouring of God's grace upon them.

B. SHORTER RITE OF BAPTISM

20. In the shorter rite of baptism designed for the use of catechists,[3] the reception of the children, the celebration of the word of God, or the instruction by the minister, and the general intercessions are retained. Before the font, the minister offers a prayer invoking God and recalling the history of salvation as it relates to baptism. After the baptismal

---

[3] See II Vatican Council, Constitution on the Sacred Liturgy, *Sacrosanctum Concilium,* 68.

washing, an adapted formulary is recited in place of the anointing with chrism, and the whole rite concludes in the customary way. The omissions, therefore, are the exorcism, the anointing with oil of catechumens and with chrism, and the *ephphetha* rite.

21. The shorter rite for baptizing a child in danger of death and in the absence of the ordinary minister has a twofold structure:

1) At the moment of death or when there is urgency because of imminent danger of death, the minister,[4] omitting all other ceremonies, pours water (not necessarily blessed but real and natural water) on the head of the child and pronounces the customary formulary.[5]

2) If, however, it is prudently judged that there is sufficient time, several of the faithful may be gathered together and, if one of them is able to lead the others in a short prayer, the following rite may be used: an explanation by the minister of the sacrament, a short set of general intercessions, the profession of faith by the parents or one godparent and the pouring of the water with the customary words. But if those present are uneducated, the minister of the sacrament should recite the profession of faith aloud and baptize according to the rite for use in danger of death.

22. In danger of death, the priest or deacon may also use this shorter form if necessary. If there is time and he has the sacred chrism, the pastor or other priest enjoying the same faculty should not fail to confer confirmation after baptism. In this case he omits the postbaptismal anointing with chrism.

V. ADAPTATIONS BY CONFERENCES OF BISHOPS OR BY BISHOPS

23. In addition to the adaptations provided for in the General Introduction (nos. 30–33, page 7), the baptismal rite for infants admits other variations, to be determined by the conferences of bishops.

24. As is indicated in the Roman Ritual, the following matters are left to the discretion of the conferences:

1) As local customs may dictate, the questioning about the name of the child may be arranged in different ways: the name may have been given already or may be given during the rite of baptism.

2) The anointing with oil of catechumens may be omitted (nos. 50, 87).

3) The formulary of renunciation may be made more pointed and detailed (nos. 57, 94, 121).

---

[4] See General Introduction, 16, page 5 above.
[5] See ibid., 23, page 6 above.

4) If the number to be baptized is very great, the anointing with chrism may be omitted (no. 125).

5) The *ephphetha* rite may be retained (nos. 65, 101).

25. In many countries parents are sometimes not ready for the celebration of baptism or they ask for their children to be baptized even though the latter will not afterward receive a Christian education and will even lose the faith. Since to instruct such parents and to inquire about their faith in the course of the rite itself is not enough, conferences of bishops may issue pastoral directives, for the guidance of pastors to determine a longer interval between birth and baptism.

26. It is for the bishop to decide for his diocese whether catechists may give the homily on their own or only by reading a written text.

VI. ADAPTATIONS BY THE MINISTER

27. During meetings to prepare the parents for the baptism of their children, it is important that the instruction should be supported by prayer and religious rites. For this the various elements provided in the rite of baptism for the celebration of the word of God will prove helpful.

28. When the baptism of children is celebrated as part of the Easter Vigil, the ritual should be arranged as follows:

1) At a convenient time and place before the Easter Vigil the rite of receiving the children is celebrated. The liturgy of the word may be omitted at the end, according to circumstances, and the prayer of exorcism is said, followed by the anointing with oil of catechumens. [See pages 21–23 and 28–31, or 51–53 and 58–59, or 73–74 and 77.]

2) The celebration of the sacrament (nos. 56–58, 60–63, pages 38–40, 41–42) takes place after the blessing of the water, as is indicated in the Rite of the Easter Vigil. [See also nos. 93–95, 97–99, pages 61–65, or nos. 120–122, 124–126, pages 80–81, 82–84.]

3) The assent of the celebrant and community (no. 59) is omitted, as are the presentation of the lighted candle (no. 64) and the *ephphetha* rite (no. 65).

4) The conclusion of the rite (nos. 67–71) is omitted.

29. If baptism takes place during Sunday Mass, the Mass for that Sunday is used, or, on the Sundays of the Christmas season and of Ordinary Time, the Mass for the Baptism of Children, and the celebration takes place as follows:

1) The rite of receiving the children (nos. 33–43, pages 21–24) takes place at the beginning of Mass and the greeting and penitential rite of the Mass are omitted. [See also nos. 73–80, pages 51–53, or nos. 107–111, pages 73–74.]

2) In the liturgy of the word:

a) The readings are taken from the Mass of the Sunday. But in the Christmas season and in Ordinary Time they may also be taken from those given in the Lectionary for Mass (III, 474–489) [English edition (1969), Readings nos. 757–761] or in this baptismal rite (nos. 44, 186–215).

When a ritual Mass is prohibited, one of the readings may be taken from the texts provided for the celebration of baptism for children, with attention paid to the pastoral benefit of the faithful and the character of the liturgical day.

b) The homily is based on the sacred texts, but should take account of the baptism that is to take place.

c) The *Credo* is not said, since the profession of faith by the entire community before baptism takes its place.

d) The general intercessions are taken from those used in the rite of baptism (nos. 47–48, page 27–28). At the end, however, before the invocation of the saints, petitions are added for the universal Church and the needs of the world. [See also nos. 84–85, 114, 217–220, pages 56–58, 76, 151–154.]

3) The celebration of baptism continues with the prayer of exorcism, anointing, and other ceremonies described in the rite (nos. 49–66, pages 28–43). [See also nos. 86–101, pages 58–66, or nos. 115–127, pages 77–84.]

4) After the celebration of baptism, the Mass continues in the usual way with the presentation of the gifts.

5) For the blessing at the end of Mass, the priest may use one of the formularies provided in the rite of baptism (nos. 70, 247–249, pages 45, 162–164). [See also nos. 105, 130, pages 68, 86.]

30. If baptism is celebrated during Mass on weekdays, it is arranged in basically the same way as on Sunday, but the readings for the liturgy of the word may be taken from those that are provided in the rite of baptism (nos. 44, 186–215, pages 24, 131–150).

31. In accordance with the General Introduction no. 34 (page 8 above), the minister may make some adaptations in the rite as circumstances require, such as:

1) If the child's mother died in childbirth, this should be taken into account in the opening instruction (no. 36, page 21), general intercessions (nos. 47, 217–220, pages 27, 151–154), and final blessing (nos. 70, 247–248, pages 45, 162–163).

2) In the dialogue with the parents (nos. 37–38, 76–77, pages 22, 52), their answers should be taken into account: if they have not answered *Baptism,* but *Faith,* or *The grace of Christ,* or *Entrance into the*

Church, or *Everlasting life,* then the minister does not begin by saying *Baptism,* but uses *Faith,* or *The grace of Christ,* and so forth.

3) The rite of bringing a child already baptized to the church (nos. 165–185, pages 113–128), which has been drawn up for use only when the child has been baptized in danger of death, should be adapted to cover other contingencies, for example, when children have been baptized during a time of religious persecution or temporary disagreement between the parents.

RITE OF BAPTISM
FOR SEVERAL CHILDREN

CHAPTER I
RITE OF BAPTISM FOR SEVERAL CHILDREN

RECEPTION OF THE CHILDREN

32. If possible, baptism should take place on Sunday, the day on which the Church celebrates the paschal mystery. It should be conferred in a communal celebration for all the recently born children, and in the presence of the faithful, or at least of relatives, friends, and neighbors, who are all to take an active part in the rite.

33. It is the role of the father and mother, accompanied by the godparents, to present the child to the Church for baptism.

34. If there are very many children, and if there are several priests or deacons present, these may help the celebrant in the parts referred to below.

35. The people may sing a psalm or hymn suitable for the occasion. Meanwhile the celebrating priest or deacon, vested in alb or surplice, with a stole (with or without a cope) of festive color, and accompanied by the ministers, goes to the entrance of the church or to that part of the church where the parents and godparents are waiting with those who are to be baptized.

36. The celebrant greets all present, and especially the parents and godparents, reminding them briefly of the joy with which the parents welcomed their children as gifts from God, the source of life, who now wishes to bestow his own life on these little ones.

37. First the celebrant questions the parents of each child.

Celebrant:

What name do you give your child? (or: **have you given?**)

Parents:

N.

Celebrant:

What do you ask of God's Church for N.**?**

Parents:

Baptism.

The celebrant may choose other words for this dialogue.

The first reply may be given by someone other than the parents if local custom gives him the right to name the child.

In the second response the parents may use other words, e.g., **faith** or **the grace of Christ** or **entrance into the Church** or **eternal life.**

38. If there are many children to be baptized, the celebrant asks the names from all the parents together, and each family replies in turn. The second question may also be asked of all together.

Celebrant:

What name do you give each of these children? (or: **have you given?**)

Parents:

N., N., etc.

Celebrant:

What do you ask of God's Church for your children?

All:

Baptism.

39. The celebrant speaks to the parents in these or similar words:

You have asked to have your children baptized. In doing so you are accepting the responsibility of training them in the practice of the faith. It will be your duty to bring them up to keep God's commandments as Christ

taught us, by loving God and our neighbor. Do you clearly understand what you are undertaking?

Parents:

We do.

This response is given by each family individually. But if there are many children to be baptized, the response may be given by all together.

40. Then the celebrant turns to the godparents and addresses them in these or similar words:

Are you ready to help these parents in their duty as Christian mothers and fathers?

All the godparents:

We are.

41. The celebrant continues:

N. and N. (or: **My dear children**), **the Christian community welcomes you with great joy. In its name I claim you for Christ our Savior by the sign of his cross. I now trace the cross on your foreheads, and invite your parents (and godparents) to do the same.**

He signs each child on the forehead, in silence. Then he invites the parents and, if it seems appropriate, the godparents to do the same.

42. The celebrant invites the parents, godparents, and the others to take part in the liturgy of the word. If circumstances permit, there is a procession to the place where this will be celebrated, during which a song is sung, e.g., Psalm 84:7, 8, 9ab:

Will you not give us life;
> **and shall not your people rejoice in you?**
Show us, O Lord, your kindness,
> **and grant us your salvation.**
I will hear what God proclaims;
> **the Lord—for he proclaims peace to his people.**

43. The children to be baptized may be carried to a separate place, where they remain until the end of the liturgy of the word.

LITURGY OF THE WORD

Scriptural Readings and Homily

44. One or even two of the following gospel passages are read, during which all may sit if convenient.

1   John 3:1-6

A reading from the holy Gospel according to John

No one can see the Kingdom of God without being born from above.

**There was a Pharisee named Nicodemus, a ruler of
    the Jews.**
He came to Jesus at night and said to him,
    **"Rabbi, we know that you are a teacher who has
        come from God,**
    for no one can do these signs that you are doing
    unless God is with him."
Jesus answered and said to him,
    "Amen, amen, I say to you,
    unless one is born from above,
    he cannot see the Kingdom of God."
Nicodemus said to him,
    "How can a man once grown old be born again?
**Surely he cannot reenter his mother's womb and be
    born again, can he?"**
Jesus answered,
    "Amen, amen, I say to you,
    unless one is born of water and Spirit
    he cannot enter the Kingdom of God.
What is born of flesh is flesh
    and what is born of spirit is spirit."

The Gospel of the Lord.

2

A reading from the holy Gospel according to Matthew

Go, therefore, and make disciples of all nations, baptizing them in the name of the Father, and of the Son, and of the Holy Spirit.

Jesus said to the Eleven disciples:

"All power in heaven and on earth has been given to me.
Go, therefore, and make disciples of all nations,
> **baptizing them in the name of the Father,**
> **and of the Son, and of the Holy Spirit,**
> **teaching them to observe all that I have commanded**
>> **you.**

And behold, I am with you always, until the end of the
> **age."**

The Gospel of the Lord.

3

A reading from the holy Gospel according to Mark

Jesus was baptized in the Jordan by John.

Jesus came from Nazareth of Galilee
> **and was baptized in the Jordan by John.**
On coming up out of the water he saw the heavens
> **being torn open**
> **and the Spirit, like a dove, descending upon him.**
And a voice came from the heavens,
> **"You are my beloved Son; with you I am well**
>> **pleased."**

The Gospel of the Lord.

4 Mark 10:13-16

A reading from the holy Gospel according to Mark

Let the children come to me; do not prevent them.

People were bringing children to Jesus that he might touch them,

but the disciples rebuked them.

When Jesus saw this he became indignant and said to them,

"Let the children come to me; do not prevent them,

for the Kingdom of God belongs to such as these.

Amen, I say to you,

whoever does not accept the Kingdom of God like a child

will not enter it."

Then he embraced them and blessed them,

placing his hands on them.

The Gospel of the Lord.

The passages listed in nos. 186–194 and 204–215 may be chosen, or other passages which better meet the wishes or needs of the parents. Between the readings, responsorial psalms or verses may be sung as given in nos. 195–203. See pages 138–142.

45. After the reading, the celebrant gives a short homily, explaining to those present the significance of what has been read. His purpose will be to lead them to a deeper understanding of the mystery of baptism and to encourage the parents and godparents to a ready acceptance of the responsibilities which arise from the sacrament.

46. After the homily, or in the course of or after the litany, it is desirable to have a period of silence while all pray at the invitation of the celebrant. If convenient, a suitable song follows, e.g., one chosen from nos. 225–245, pages 159–161.

[If baptism is to be celebrated at Sunday or weekday Mass, the Order of Mass begins here with the **Lord, have mercy.**]

GENERAL INTERCESSIONS

47. Then the general intercessions are said:

Celebrant:

My brothers and sisters,* let us ask our Lord Jesus Christ to look lovingly on these children who are to be baptized, on their parents and godparents, and on all the baptized.

Leader:

By the mystery of your death and resurrection, bathe these children in light, give them the new life of baptism and welcome them into your holy Church.

All:

Lord, hear our prayer.

Leader:

Through baptism and confirmation, make them your faithful followers and witnesses to your gospel.

All:

Lord, hear our prayer.

Leader:

Lead them by a holy life to the joys of God's kingdom.

All:

Lord, hear our prayer.

Leader:

Make the lives of their parents and godparents examples of faith to inspire these children.

All:

Lord, hear our prayer.

Leader:

Keep their families always in your love.

All:

Lord, hear our prayer.

---

*At the discretion of the priest, other words which seem more suitable under the circumstances, such as **friends** or **dearly beloved** or **brethren**, may be used. This also applies to parallel instances in the liturgy.

Leader:

Renew the grace of our baptism in each one of us.

All:

Lord, hear our prayer.

Other forms may be chosen from nos. 217–220, pages **151–154**.

48. The celebrant next invites all present to invoke the saints. At this point, if the children have been taken out, they are brought back.

Holy Mary, Mother of God,	**pray for us.**
Saint John the Baptist,	**pray for us.**
Saint Joseph,	**pray for us.**
Saint Peter and Saint Paul,	**pray for us.**

The names of other saints may be added, especially the patrons of the children to be baptized, and of the church or locality. The litany concludes:

All holy men and women,	**pray for us.**

PRAYER OF EXORCISM AND ANOINTING BEFORE BAPTISM

49. After the invocations, the celebrant says:

A **Almighty and ever-living God,**
you sent your only Son into the world
to cast out the power of Satan, spirit of evil,
to rescue man from the kingdom of darkness,
and bring him into the splendor of your kingdom of light.
We pray for these children:
set them free from original sin,
make them temples of your glory,
and send your Holy Spirit to dwell within them.
(We ask this) through Christ our Lord.

All:

Amen.

Another form of the prayer of exorcism

B **Almighty God,**
you sent your only Son
to rescue us from the slavery of sin,
and to give us the freedom
only your sons and daughters enjoy.
We now pray for these children
who will have to face the world with its temptations,
and fight the devil in all his cunning.
Your Son died and rose again to save us.
By his victory over sin and death,
cleanse these children from the stain of original sin.
Strengthen them with the grace of Christ,
and watch over them at every step in life's journey.
(We ask this) through Christ our Lord.

All:
Amen.

50. The celebrant continues:

We anoint you with the oil of salvation
in the name of Christ our Savior;
may he strengthen you
with his power,
who lives and reigns for ever and ever.

All:
Amen.

He anoints each child on the breast with the oil of catechumens.
If the number of children is large, the anointing may be done
by several ministers.

51. If, for serious reasons, the conference of bishops so decides, the anointing before baptism may be omitted. [In the United States, it may be omitted only when the minister of baptism judges the omission to be pastorally necessary or desirable.] In that case the celebrant says once only:

May you have strength in the power of Christ our Savior, who lives and reigns for ever and ever.

All:

Amen.

And immediately he lays his hand on each child in silence.

52. If the baptistery is located outside the church or is not within view of the congregation, all go there in procession.

If the baptistery is located within view of the congregation, the celebrant, parents, and godparents go there with the children, while the others remain in their places.

If, however, the baptistery cannot accommodate the congregation, the baptism may be celebrated in a suitable place within the church, and the parents and godparents bring the child forward at the proper moment.

Meanwhile, if it can be done suitably, an appropriate song is sung, e.g., Psalm 23:

The LORD is my shepherd; I shall not want.
   In verdant pastures he gives me repose;
Beside restful waters he leads me;
   he refreshes my soul.
He guides me in right paths
   for his name's sake.
Even though I walk in the dark valley
   I fear no evil; for you are at my side
With your rod and your staff
   that give me courage.
You spread the table before me
   in the sight of my foes,

You anoint my head with oil;
>   my cup overflows.
Only goodness and kindness follow me
>   all the days of my life;
And I shall dwell in the house of the LORD
>   for years to come.

CELEBRATION OF THE SACRAMENT

53. When they come to the font, the celebrant briefly reminds the congregation of the wonderful work of God whose plan it is to sanctify man, body and soul, through water. He may use these or similar words:

A   **My dear brothers and sisters, we now ask God to give these children new life in abundance through water and the Holy Spirit.**

or:

B   **My dear brothers and sisters, God uses the sacrament of water to give his divine life to those who believe in him. Let us turn to him, and ask him to pour his gift of life from this font on the children he has chosen.**

BLESSING AND INVOCATION OF GOD OVER BAPTISMAL WATER

54. Then, turning to the font, he sings or says the following blessing (outside the Easter season):

Fa-ther, you give us grace through sac-ra-men-tal signs, which tell us of the won-ders of your un-seen power. In baptism we use your gift of wa-ter, which you have made a rich sym-bol of the grace you give us in this sac-ra-ment. At the very dawn of creation your Spirit breathed on the wa-ters, making them the well-spring of all ho-li-ness. The waters of the great flood you made a sign of the wa-ters of bap-tism, that make an end of sin and a new be-gin-ning of good-ness. Through the waters of the Red Sea you led Is-ra-el out of slav-ery, to be an image of God's ho-ly peo-ple, set free from sin by bap-tism. In the waters of the Jordan your Son was bap-tized by John and a-noint-ed with the Spir-it. Your Son willed that water and blood should flow from his side as he hung up-on the cross. After his resurrection he told his dis-ci-ples:

"Go out and teach all na-tions, baptizing them in the name of the Father,

and of the Son and of the Ho - ly Spir-it." Fa-ther, look now with love

up - on your Church, and un-seal for her the foun - tain of bap - tism.

By the power of the Ho - ly Spir - it give to the wa-ter of this font

the grace of your Son. You cre-ated man in your own like-ness: cleanse him

from sin in a new birth of in-no-cence by wa-ter and the Spir-it.

The celebrant touches the water with his right hand and continues:

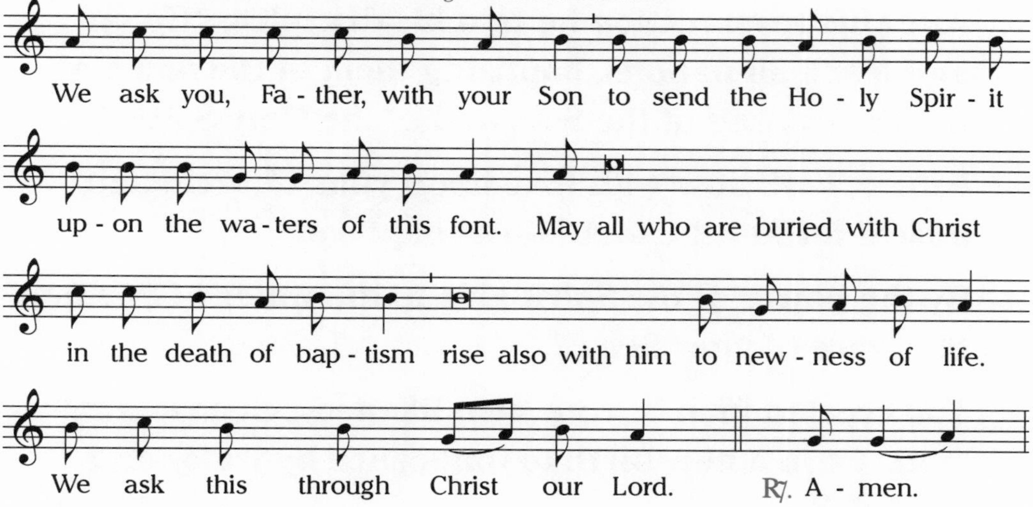

We ask you, Fa - ther, with your Son to send the Ho - ly Spir - it

up - on the wa-ters of this font. May all who are buried with Christ

in the death of bap - tism rise also with him to new - ness of life.

We ask this through Christ our Lord. ℟. A - men.

Acclamation:

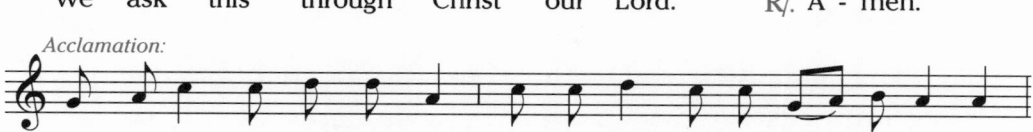

Springs of wa - ter, bless the Lord. Give him glo - ry and praise for ev - er.

A   **Father, you give us grace through sacramental signs, which tell us of the wonders of your unseen power.**

In baptism we use your gift of water, which you have made a rich symbol of the grace you give us in this sacrament.

At the very dawn of creation your Spirit breathed on the waters, making them the wellspring of all holiness.

The waters of the great flood you made a sign of the waters of baptism, that make an end of sin and a new beginning of goodness.

Through the waters of the Red Sea you led Israel out of slavery, to be an image of God's holy people, set free from sin by baptism.

In the waters of the Jordan your Son was baptized by John and anointed with the Spirit.

Your Son willed that water and blood should flow from his side as he hung upon the cross.

After his resurrection he told his disciples: "Go out and teach all nations, baptizing them in the name of the Father, and of the Son, and of the Holy Spirit."

Father, look now with love upon your Church, and unseal for her the fountain of baptism.

By the power of the Spirit give to the water of this font the grace of your Son.

You created man in your own likeness: cleanse him from sin in a new birth to innocence by water and the Spirit.

The celebrant touches the water with his right hand and continues:

We ask you, Father, with your Son to send the Holy Spirit upon the water of this font. May all who are buried with Christ in the death of baptism rise also with him to newness of life. We ask this through Christ our Lord.

All:

Amen.

Other forms of the blessing:

B   Celebrant:

Praise to you, almighty God and Father, for you have created water to cleanse and to give life.

All:

Blessed be God (or some other suitable acclamation by the people).

Celebrant:

Praise to you, Lord Jesus Christ, the Father's only Son, for you offered yourself on the cross, that in the blood and water flowing from your side, and through your death and resurrection, the Church might be born.

All:

Blessed be God.

Celebrant:

Praise to you, God the Holy Spirit, for you anointed Christ at his baptism in the waters of Jordan, so that we might all be baptized into you.

All:

Blessed be God.

Celebrant:

* Come to us, Lord, Father of all, and make holy this water which you have created, so that all who are baptized in it may be washed clean of sin, and be born again to live as your children.

All:

Hear us, Lord (or some other suitable invocation).

Celebrant:

Make this water holy, Lord, so that all who are baptized into Christ's death and resurrection by this water may become more perfectly like your Son.

All:

Hear us, Lord.

The celebrant touches the water with his right hand and continues:

Lord, make holy this water which you have created, so that all those whom you have chosen may be born again by the power of the Holy Spirit, and may take their place among your holy people.

All:

Hear us, Lord.

* If the baptismal water has already been blessed, the celebrant omits the invocation Come to us, Lord and those which follow it, and says:

You have called your children, N., N., to this cleansing water that they may share in the faith of your Church and have eternal life. By the mystery of this consecrated water lead them to a new and spiritual birth. We ask this through Christ our Lord.

All:

Amen.

C Celebrant:

Father, God of mercy, through these waters of baptism you have filled us with new life as your very own children.

All:

Blessed be God (or some other suitable acclamation by the people).

Celebrant:

From all who are baptized in water and the Holy Spirit, you have formed one people, united in your Son Jesus Christ.

All:

Blessed be God.

Celebrant:

You have set us free and filled our hearts with the Spirit of your love, that we may live in your peace.

All:

Blessed be God.

Celebrant:

You call those who have been baptized to announce the Good News of Jesus Christ to people everywhere.

All:

Blessed be God.

Celebrant:

* You have called your children, N., N., to this cleansing water and new birth that by sharing the faith of your Church they might have eternal life. Bless ✝ this water in which they will be baptized. We ask this in the name of Christ our Lord.

All:

Amen.

> * If the baptismal water has already been blessed, the celebrant omits this last prayer and says:
>
> **You have called your children, N., N., to this cleansing water that they may share in the faith of your Church and have eternal life. By the mystery of this consecrated water lead them to a new and spiritual birth. We ask this through Christ our Lord.**
>
> All:
> **Amen.**

55. During the Easter season, if there is baptismal water which was consecrated at the Easter Vigil, the blessing and invocation of God over the water are nevertheless included, so that this theme of thanksgiving and petition may find a place in the baptism. The forms of this blessing and invocation are those found in nos. 223–224 (B and C above), with the variation indicated at the end of each text.

Renunciation of Sin and Profession of Faith

56. The celebrant speaks to the parents and godparents in these words:

Dear parents and godparents: You have come here to present these children for baptism. By water and the Holy Spirit they are to receive the gift of new life from God, who is love.

On your part, you must make it your constant care to bring them up in the practice of the faith. See that the divine life which God gives them is kept safe from the poison of sin, to grow always stronger in their hearts.

If your faith makes you ready to accept this responsibility, renew now the vows of your own baptism. Reject sin; profess your faith in Christ Jesus. This is the faith of the Church. This is the faith in which these children are about to be baptized.

57. The celebrant questions the parents and godparents.

A   Celebrant:

Do you reject Satan?

Parents and godparents:
I do.

Celebrant:

And all his works?

Parents and godparents:
I do.

Celebrant:

And all his empty promises?

Parents and godparents:
I do.

or:

B   Celebrant:

Do you reject sin, so as to live in the freedom of God's children?

Parents and godparents:
I do.

Celebrant:

Do you reject the glamor of evil, and refuse to be mastered by sin?

Parents and godparents:
I do.

Celebrant:

Do you reject Satan, father of sin and prince of darkness?

Parents and godparents:
I do.

According to circumstances, this second form may be expressed with greater precision by the conferences of bishops, especially in places where it is necessary for the parents and godparents to reject superstitious and magical practices used with children.

58. Next the celebrant asks for the threefold profession of faith from the parents and godparents:

Celebrant:

Do you believe in God, the Father almighty, creator of heaven and earth?

Parents and godparents:

I do.

Celebrant:

Do you believe in Jesus Christ, his only Son, our Lord, who was born of the Virgin Mary, was crucified, died, and was buried, rose from the dead, and is now seated at the right hand of the Father?

Parents and godparents:

I do.

Celebrant:

Do you believe in the Holy Spirit, the holy catholic Church, the communion of saints, the forgiveness of sins, the resurrection of the body, and life everlasting?

Parents and godparents:

I do.

[If the baptism is celebrated during the Easter Vigil, the rite continues with no. 60 below.]

59. The celebrant and the congregation give their assent to this profession of faith:

Celebrant:

This is our faith. This is the faith of the Church. We are proud to profess it, in Christ Jesus our Lord.

All:

Amen.

If desired, some other formula may be used instead, or a suitable song by which the community expresses its faith with a single voice.

BAPTISM

60. The celebrant invites the first of the families to the font. Using the name of the individual child, he questions the parents and godparents.

Celebrant:

Is it your will that N. should be baptized in the faith of the Church, which we have all professed with you?

Parents and godparents:

It is.

He baptizes the child, saying:

N., I baptize you in the name of the Father,

He immerses the child or pours water upon it.

and of the Son,

He immerses the child or pours water upon it a second time.

and of the Holy Spirit.

He immerses the child or pours water upon it a third time.

He asks the same question and performs the same action for each child.

After each baptism it is appropriate for the people to sing a short acclamation. (See nos. 225–245, pages **159–161**.)

If the baptism is performed by the pouring of water, it is preferable that the child be held by the mother (or father). Where, however, it is felt that the existing custom should be retained, the godmother (or godfather) may hold the child. If baptism is by immersion, the mother or father (godmother or godfather) lifts the child out of the font.

61. If the number of children to be baptized is large, and other priests or deacons are present, these may baptize some of the children in the way described above, and with the same form.

EXPLANATORY RITES

ANOINTING AFTER BAPTISM

62. Then the celebrant says:

God the Father of our Lord Jesus Christ has freed you from sin, given you a new birth by water and the Holy Spirit, and welcomed you into his holy people. He now anoints you with the chrism of salvation. As Christ was anointed Priest, Prophet, and King, so may you live always as members of his body, sharing everlasting life.

All:

Amen.

Next, the celebrant anoints each child on the crown of the head with chrism, in silence.

If the number of children is large and other priests or deacons are present, these may anoint some of the children with chrism.

CLOTHING WITH WHITE GARMENT

63. The celebrant says:

(N. and N.), you have become a new creation, and have clothed yourselves in Christ.

See in this white garment the outward sign of your Christian dignity. With your family and friends to help you by word and example, bring that dignity unstained into the everlasting life of heaven.

All:

Amen.

The white garments are put on the children. A different color is not permitted unless demanded by local custom. It is desirable that the families provide the garments.

[If baptism is celebrated during the Easter Vigil, the rite of baptism ends here, and the rite of the Easter Vigil continues.]

LIGHTED CANDLE

64. The celebrant takes the Easter candle and says:

Receive the light of Christ.

Someone from each family (e.g., the father or godfather) lights the child's candle from the Easter candle.

The celebrant then says:

Parents and godparents, this light is entrusted to you to be kept burning brightly. These children of yours have been enlightened by Christ. They are to walk always as children of the light. May they keep the flame of faith alive in their hearts. When the Lord comes, may they go out to meet him with all the saints in the heavenly kingdom.

EPHPHETHA OR PRAYER OVER EARS AND MOUTH

65. If the conference of bishops decides to preserve the practice, the rite of *Ephphetha* follows. [In the United States it may be performed at the discretion of the minister.] The celebrant touches the ears and mouth of each child with his thumb, saying:

The Lord Jesus made the deaf hear and the dumb speak. May he soon touch your ears to receive his word, and your mouth to proclaim his faith, to the praise and glory of God the Father.

All:

Amen.

66. If the number of children is large, the celebrant says the formula once, but does not touch the ears and mouth.

[If baptism is celebrated during Sunday or weekday Mass, the Mass continues in the usual way with the offertory.]

CONCLUSION OF THE RITE

67. Next there is a procession to the altar, unless the baptism was performed in the sanctuary. The lighted candles are carried for the children.

A baptismal song is appropriate at this time, e.g.:

You have put on Christ,
in him you have been baptized.
Alleluia, alleluia.

Other songs may be chosen from nos. 225–245, pages 159–161.

LORD'S PRAYER

68. The celebrant stands in front of the altar and addresses the parents, godparents, and the whole assembly in these or similar words:

Dearly beloved, these children have been reborn in
baptism. They are now called children of God, for so
indeed they are. In confirmation they will receive the
fullness of God's Spirit. In holy communion they will
share the banquet of Christ's sacrifice, calling God their
Father in the midst of the Church. In their name, in the
Spirit of our common sonship, let us pray together in
the words our Lord has given us:

69. All present join the celebrant in singing or saying:

Our Father,
who art in heaven,
hallowed be thy name;
thy kingdom come;
thy will be done on earth as it is in heaven.
Give us this day our daily bread;
and forgive us our trespasses
as we forgive those who trespass against us;
and lead us not into temptation,
but deliver us from evil.

Blessing and Dismissal

70. The celebrant first blesses mothers, who hold the children in their arms, then the fathers, and lastly the entire assembly:

A   Celebrant:

God the Father, through his Son, the Virgin Mary's child, has brought joy to all Christian mothers, as they see the hope of eternal life shine on their children. May he bless the mothers of these children. They now thank God for the gift of their children. May they be one with them in thanking him for ever in heaven, in Christ Jesus our Lord.

All:

Amen.

Celebrant:

God is the giver of all life, human and divine. May he bless the fathers of these children. With their wives they will be the first teachers of their children in the ways of faith. May they be also the best of teachers, bearing witness to the faith by what they say and do, in Christ Jesus our Lord.

All:

Amen.

Celebrant:

By God's gift, through water and the Holy Spirit, we are reborn to everlasting life. In his goodness, may he continue to pour out his blessings upon all present, who are his sons and daughters. May he make them always, wherever they may be, faithful members of his holy people. May he send his peace upon all who are gathered here, in Christ Jesus our Lord.

All:

Amen.

Celebrant:

May almighty God, the Father, and the Son, ✝ and the Holy Spirit, bless you.

All:

Amen.

Celebrant:

Go in peace.

All:

Thanks be to God.

Other forms of the final blessing:

B   Celebrant:

May God the almighty Father, who filled the world with joy by giving us his only Son, bless these newly-baptized children. May they grow to be more fully like Jesus Christ our Lord.

All:

Amen.

Celebrant:

May almighty God, who gives life on earth and in heaven, bless the parents of these children. They thank him now for the gift he has given them. May they always show that gratitude in action by loving and caring for their children.

All:

Amen.

Celebrant:

May almighty God, who has given us a new birth by water and the Holy Spirit, generously bless all of us who are his faithful children. May we always live as his people, and may he bless all here present with his peace.

All:

Amen.

Celebrant:

May almighty God, the Father, and the Son, ☩ and the Holy Spirit, bless you.

All:

Amen.

Celebrant:

Go in peace.

All:

Thanks be to God.

C   Celebrant:

May God, the source of life and love, who fills the hearts of mothers with love for their children, bless the mothers of these newly-baptized children. As they thank God for a safe delivery, may they find joy in the love, growth, and holiness of their children.

All:

Amen.

Celebrant:

May God, the Father and model of all fathers, help these fathers to give good example, so that their children will grow to be mature Christians in all the fullness of Jesus Christ.

All:

Amen.

Celebrant:

May God, who loves all people, bless all the relatives and friends who are gathered here. In his mercy, may he guard them from evil and give them his abundant peace.

All:

Amen.

Celebrant:

And may almighty God, the Father, and the Son, ✠ and the Holy Spirit, bless you.

All:

Amen.

Celebrant:

Go in peace.

All:

Thanks be to God.

D Celebrant:

My brothers and sisters, we entrust you all to the mercy and help of God the almighty Father, his only Son, and the Holy Spirit. May he watch over your life, and may we all walk by the light of faith, and attain the good things he has promised us.

Go in peace, and may almighty God, the Father, and the Son, ✠ and the Holy Spirit, bless you.

All:

Amen.

Celebrant:

And may almighty God, the Father, and the Son, ✠ and the Holy Spirit, bless you.

All:

Amen.

Celebrant:

Go in peace.

All:

Thanks be to God.

71. After the blessing, all may sing a hymn which suitably expresses thanksgiving and Easter joy, or they may sing the song of the Blessed Virgin Mary, the Magnificat.

Where there is the practice of bringing baptized infants to the altar of the Blessed Virgin Mary, this custom is observed if appropriate.

RITE OF BAPTISM
FOR ONE CHILD

CHAPTER II
RITE OF BAPTISM FOR ONE CHILD

RECEPTION OF THE CHILD

72. If possible, baptism should take place on Sunday, the day on which the Church celebrates the paschal mystery. It should be conferred in a communal celebration in the presence of the faithful, or at least of relatives, friends, and neighbors, who are all to take an active part in the rite.

73. It is the role of the father and mother, accompanied by the godparents, to present the child to the Church for baptism.

74. The people may sing a psalm or hymn suitable for the occasion. Meanwhile the celebrating priest or deacon, vested in alb or surplice, with a stole (with or without a cope) of festive color, and accompanied by the ministers goes to the entrance of the church or to that part of the church where the parents and godparents are waiting with the child.

75. The celebrant greets all present, and especially the parents and godparents, reminding them briefly of the joy with which the parents welcomed this child as a gift from God, the source of life, who now wishes to bestow his own life on this little one.

+ exciting generous Door

76. First the celebrant questions the parents:

Celebrant:

What name do you give your child? (or: **have you given?**)

Parents:

N. Saint

Celebrant:

What do you ask of God's Church for N.**?**

Parents:

Baptism.

The celebrant may choose other words for this dialogue.

The first reply may be given by someone other than the parents if local custom gives him the right to name the child.

In the second response the parents may use other words, e.g., faith or the grace of Christ or entrance into the Church or eternal life.

77. The celebrant speaks to the parents in these or similar words:

Catech. New Rite

Village raises

You have asked to have your child baptized. In doing so you are accepting the responsibility of training him (**her**) **in the practice of the faith. It will be your duty to bring him** (**her**) **up to keep God's commandments as Christ taught us, by loving God and our neighbor. Do you clearly understand what you are undertaking?**

Parents:

We do.

78. Then the celebrant turns to the godparents and addresses them in these or similar words:

Are you ready to help the parents of this child in their duty as Christian parents?

Godparents:

We are.

79. The celebrant continues:

N., the Christian community welcomes you with great joy. In its name I claim you for Christ our Savior by the sign of his cross. I now trace the cross on your forehead, and invite your parents (and godparents) to do the same.

He signs the child on the forehead, in silence. Then he invites the parents and (if it seems appropriate) the godparents to do the same.

only hope   go ⌐ Let us pray →
                ⌐ Gloria   *or*
                                              Ps. 148

80. The celebrant invites the parents, godparents, and the others to take part in the liturgy of the word. If circumstances permit, there is a procession to the place where this will be celebrated, during which a song is sung, e.g., Psalm 84:7, 8, 9ab:

Will you not give us life;
    and shall not your people rejoice in you?
Show us, O Lord, your kindness,
    and grant us your salvation.
I will hear what God proclaims;
    the Lord—for he proclaims peace to his people.

[If baptism is to be celebrated at Sunday or weekday Mass, the Order of Mass begins here with the **Lord, have mercy.**]

LITURGY OF THE WORD

Pg. 148   Gos.
then Pg. 57

SCRIPTURAL READINGS AND HOMILY

81. One or even two of the following gospel passages are read, during which all may sit if convenient.

1   John 3:1-6

> **A reading from the holy Gospel according to John**
> *No one can see the Kingdom of God without being born from above.*
>
> **There was a Pharisee named Nicodemus, a ruler of
>   the Jews.**
> **He came to Jesus at night and said to him,**
>   **"Rabbi, we know that you are a teacher who has
>   come from God,**
>   **for no one can do these signs that you are doing
>   unless God is with him."**
> **Jesus answered and said to him,**
>   **"Amen, amen, I say to you,**
>   **unless one is born from above,**
>   **he cannot see the Kingdom of God."**
> **Nicodemus said to him,**
>   **"How can a man once grown old be born again?**
> **Surely he cannot reenter his mother's womb and be
>   born again, can he?"**
> **Jesus answered,**
>   **"Amen, amen, I say to you,**
>   **unless one is born of water and Spirit**
>   **he cannot enter the Kingdom of God.**
> **What is born of flesh is flesh**
>   **and what is born of spirit is spirit."**
>
> **The Gospel of the Lord.**

2   Matthew 28:18-20

A reading from the holy Gospel according to Matthew

Go, therefore, and make disciples of all nations, baptizing them in the name of the Father, and of the Son, and of the Holy Spirit.

Jesus said to the Eleven disciples:

"All power in heaven and on earth has been given to me.

Go, therefore, and make disciples of all nations,
      baptizing them in the name of the Father,
      and of the Son, and of the Holy Spirit,
      teaching them to observe all that I have commanded
           you.

And behold, I am with you always, until the end of the
           age."

The Gospel of the Lord.

3   Mark 1:9-11

A reading from the holy Gospel according to Mark

Jesus was baptized in the Jordan by John.

Jesus came from Nazareth of Galilee
      and was baptized in the Jordan by John.

On coming up out of the water he saw the heavens
      being torn open
      and the Spirit, like a dove, descending upon him.

And a voice came from the heavens,
      "You are my beloved Son; with you I am well
           pleased."

The Gospel of the Lord.

4   Mark 10:13-16

A reading from the holy Gospel according to Mark

Let the children come to me; do not prevent them.

People were bringing children to Jesus that he might
touch them,
but the disciples rebuked them.
When Jesus saw this he became indignant and said
to them,
"Let the children come to me; do not prevent them,
for the Kingdom of God belongs to such as these.
Amen, I say to you,
whoever does not accept the Kingdom of God like
a child
will not enter it."
Then he embraced them and blessed them,
placing his hands on them.

The Gospel of the Lord.

The passages listed in nos. 186–194 and 204–215 may be
chosen, or other passages which better meet the wishes or
needs of the parents. Between the readings, responsorial
psalms or verses may be sung as given in nos. 195–203. See
pages 138–142.

82. After the reading, the celebrant gives a short homily,
explaining to those present the significance of what has been
read. His purpose will be to lead them to a deeper understanding of the mystery of baptism and to encourage the parents
and godparents to a ready acceptance of the responsibilities
which arise from the sacrament.

83. After the homily, or in the course of or after the litany, it is
desirable to have a period of silence while all pray at the invitation of the celebrant. If convenient, a suitable song follows,
such as one chosen from nos. 225–245, pages 159–161.

GENERAL INTERCESSIONS

84. Then the general intercessions are said:

Celebrant:

My dear brothers and sisters, let us ask our Lord Jesus Christ to look lovingly on this child who is to be baptized, on his (her) parents and godparents, and on all the baptized.

Leader:

By the mystery of your death and resurrection, bathe this child in light, give him (her) the new life of baptism and welcome him (her) into your holy Church.

All:

Lord, hear our prayer.

Leader:

Through baptism and confirmation, make him (her) your faithful follower and a witness to your gospel.

All:

Lord, hear our prayer.

Leader:

Lead him (her) by a holy life to the joys of God's kingdom.

All:

Lord, hear our prayer.

Leader:

Make the lives of his (her) parents and godparents examples of faith to inspire this child.

All:

Lord, hear our prayer.

Leader:

Keep his (her) family always in your love.

All:

Lord, hear our prayer.

Leader:

Renew the grace of our baptism in each one of us.

All:

Lord, hear our prayer.   *Saints* →

Other forms may be chosen from nos. 217–220, pages **151–154**.

85. The celebrant next invites all present to invoke the saints.

→ **Holy Mary, Mother of God,   pray for us.**
Saint John the Baptist,   pray for us.
Saint Joseph,   pray for us.
Saint Peter and Saint Paul, pray for us.

Patrons The names of other saints may be added, especially the patrons of the child to be baptized, and of the church or locality. The litany concludes:

All holy men and women,   pray for us.

PRAYER OF EXORCISM AND ANOINTING BEFORE BAPTISM

Catech. Pg. 155

86. After the invocation, the celebrant says:

**Almighty and ever-living God,
you sent your only Son into the world
to cast out the power of Satan, spirit of evil,
to rescue man from the kingdom of darkness,
and bring him into the splendor of your kingdom of light.
We pray for this child:
set him (her) free from original sin,
make him (her) temples of your glory,
and send your Holy Spirit to dwell with him (her).
(We ask this) through Christ our Lord.**

All:
Amen.

> *Catech.* For another form of the prayer of exorcism, see no. 221, page 155.

87. The celebrant continues: *(breast)*

O.C. **We anoint you with the oil of salvation
in the name of Christ our Savior;
may he strengthen you
with his power,
who lives and reigns for ever and ever.**

All:
Amen.

He anoints the child on the breast with the oil of catechumens.

88. If, for serious reasons, the conference of bishops so decides, the anointing before baptism may be omitted. [In the United States, it may be omitted only when the minister of baptism judges the omission to be pastorally necessary or desirable.] In that case the celebrant says:

May you have strength in the power of Christ our Savior, who lives and reigns for ever and ever.

All:

Amen.

And immediately he lays his hand on the child in silence.

89. Then they go to the baptistery, or to the sanctuary when baptism is celebrated there on occasion.

CELEBRATION OF THE SACRAMENT

90. When they come to the font, the celebrant briefly reminds the congregation of the wonderful work of God whose plan it is to sanctify man, body and soul, through water. He may use these or similar words:

A **My dear brothers and sisters, we now ask God to give this child new life in abundance through water and the Holy Spirit.**

or:

B **My dear brothers and sisters, God uses the sacrament of water to give his divine life to those who believe in him. Let us turn to him, and ask him to pour his gift of life from this font on this child he has chosen.**

BLESSING AND INVOCATION OF GOD OVER BAPTISMAL WATER

91. Then, turning to the font, he says the following blessing (<u>outside the Easter season</u>): + *Easter if not blessed*

> Father, you give us grace through sacramental signs, which tell us of the wonders of your unseen power.

In baptism we use your gift of water, which you have made a rich symbol of the grace you give us in this sacrament.

At the very dawn of creation your Spirit breathed on the waters, making them the wellspring of all holiness.

The waters of the great flood you made a sign of the waters of baptism, that make an end of sin and a new beginning of goodness.

Through the waters of the Red Sea you led Israel out of slavery, to be an image of God's holy people, set free from sin by baptism.

In the waters of the Jordan your Son was baptized by John and anointed with the Spirit.

Your Son willed that water and blood should flow from his side as he hung upon the cross.

After his resurrection he told his disciples: "Go out and teach all nations, baptizing them in the name of the Father, and of the Son, and of the Holy Spirit."

Father, look now with love upon your Church, and unseal for her the fountain of baptism.

By the power of the Spirit give to the water of this font the grace of your Son.

You created man in your own likeness: cleanse him from sin in a new birth to innocence by water and the Spirit.

The celebrant touches the water with his right hand and continues:

We ask you, Father, with your Son to send the Holy Spirit upon the water of this font. May all who are buried with Christ in the death of baptism rise also with him to newness of life. We ask this through Christ our Lord.

All:

Amen.

Other forms may be chosen from nos. 223–224, pages 156–158.

92. During the Easter season, if there is baptismal water which was consecrated at the Easter Vigil, the blessing and invocation of God over the water are nevertheless included, so that this theme of thanksgiving and petition may find a place in the baptism. The forms of this blessing and invocation are those found in nos. 223–224, pages 156–158, with the variation indicated at the end of each text.

RENUNCIATION OF SIN AND PROFESSION OF FAITH

93. The celebrant speaks to the parents and godparents in these words:

Dear parents and godparents: You have come here to present this child for baptism. By water and the Holy Spirit he (she) is to receive the gift of new life from God, who is love.

On your part, you must make it your constant care to bring him (her) up in the practice of the faith. See that the divine life which God gives him (her) is kept safe from the poison of sin, to grow always stronger in his (her) heart.

If your faith makes you ready to accept this responsibility, renew now the vows of your own baptism. Reject sin; profess your faith in Christ Jesus. This is the faith of the Church. This is the faith in which this child is about to be baptized.

94. The celebrant questions the parents and godparents.

A

Celebrant:

Do you reject Satan?

Parents and godparents:

I do.

Celebrant:

And all his works?

Parents and godparents:

I do.

Celebrant:

And all his empty promises?

Parents and godparents:

I do.

or:

B   Celebrant:

Do you reject sin, so as to live in the freedom of God's children?

Parents and godparents:

I do.

Celebrant:

Do you reject the glamor of evil, and refuse to be mastered by sin?

Parents and godparents:

I do.

Celebrant:

Do you reject Satan, father of sin and prince of darkness?

Parents and godparents:

I do.

According to circumstances, this second form may be expressed with greater precision by the conferences of bishops, especially in places where it is necessary for the parents and godparents to reject superstitious and magical practices used with children.

95. Next the celebrant asks for the threefold profession of faith from the parents and godparents:

Celebrant:

Do you believe in God, the Father almighty, creator of heaven and earth?

Parents and godparents:

I do.

Celebrant:

Do you believe in Jesus Christ, his only Son, our Lord, who was born of the Virgin Mary, was crucified, died, and was buried, rose from the dead, and is now seated at the right hand of the Father?

Parents and godparents:

I do.

Celebrant:

Do you believe in the Holy Spirit, the holy catholic Church, the communion of saints, the forgiveness of sins, the resurrection of the body, and life everlasting?

Parents and godparents:

I do.

[If the baptism is celebrated during the Easter Vigil, the rite continues with no. 97 below.]

96. The celebrant and the congregation give their assent to this profession of faith:

Celebrant:

This is our faith. This is the faith of the Church. We are proud to profess it, in Christ Jesus our Lord.

All:

Amen.

If desired, some other formula may be used instead, or a suitable song by which the community expresses its faith with a single voice.

BAPTISM

97. The celebrant invites the family to the font and <u>questions</u>
<u>the parents and godparents:</u>

Celebrant:

Is it your will that N. should be baptized in the faith of the Church, which we have all professed with you?

Parents and godparents:

It is.   *Gather*

He baptizes the child, saying:

N., I baptize you in the name of the Father,

He immerses the child or pours water upon it.

and of the Son,

He immerses the child or pours water upon it a second time.

and of the Holy Spirit.

He immerses the child or pours water upon it a third time.

After the child is baptized, it is appropriate for the people to sing a short acclamation. (See nos. 225–245, pages **159–161**.)

If the baptism is performed by the pouring of water, it is preferable that the child be held by the mother (or father). Where, however, it is felt that the existing custom should be retained, the godmother (or godfather) may hold the child. If baptism is by immersion, the mother or father (godmother or godfather) lifts the child out of the font.

At Easter. (on the Day)

God, the all-powerful Father of our Lord Jesus Christ, has given us a new birth by water and the Holy Spirit, and forgiven all our sins.

May he also keep us faithful to our Lord Jesus Christ for ever and ever.   *sprinkle   all*

EXPLANATORY RITES

ANOINTING AFTER BAPTISM

Catech.
S.C.

98. Then the celebrant says: (*head*)

God the Father of our Lord Jesus Christ has freed you from sin, given you a new birth by water and the Holy Spirit, and welcomed you into his holy people. He now anoints you with the chrism of salvation. As Christ was anointed Priest, Prophet, and King, so may you live always as a member of his body, sharing everlasting life.

All:

Amen.

Then the celebrant anoints the child on the crown of the head with the sacred chrism, in silence.

CLOTHING WITH THE WHITE GARMENT

Catech.

99. The celebrant says:

N., you have become a new creation, and have clothed yourself in Christ.

See in this white garment the outward sign of your Christian dignity. With your family and friends to help you by word and example, bring that dignity unstained into the everlasting life of heaven.

All:

Amen.

The white garment is put on the child. A different color is not permitted unless demanded by local custom. It is desirable that the family provide the garment.

[If baptism is celebrated during the Easter Vigil, the rite of baptism ends here, and the rite of the Easter Vigil continues.]

LIGHTED CANDLE

Catech

100. The celebrant takes the Easter candle and says:

Touch Pasch. Candle   hand small to G. parent

Receive the light of Christ.

> Someone from the family (such as the father or godfather) lights the child's candle from the Easter candle.

> The celebrant then says:

Parents and godparent (or: **godparents**), **this light is entrusted to you to be kept burning brightly. This child of yours has been enlightened by Christ. He (she) is to walk always as a child of the light. May he (she) keep the flame of faith alive in his (her) heart. When the Lord comes, may he (she) go out to meet him with all the saints in the heavenly kingdom.**

EPHPHETHA OR PRAYER OVER EARS AND MOUTH

> 101. If the conference of bishops decides to preserve the practice, the rite of *Ephphetha* follows. [In the United States it may be performed at the discretion of the minister.] The celebrant touches the ears and mouth of the child with his thumb, saying:

The Lord Jesus made the deaf hear and the dumb speak. May he soon touch your ears to receive his word, and your mouth to proclaim his faith, to the praise and glory of God the Father.

> All:

Amen.

Go — Light altar candles

> [If baptism is celebrated during Sunday or weekday Mass, the Mass continues in the usual way with the offertory.]

CONCLUSION OF THE RITE

> 102. Next there is a procession to the altar, unless the baptism was performed in the sanctuary. The lighted candle is carried for the child.

> A baptismal song is appropriate at this time, e.g.:

You have put on Christ,
in him you have been baptized.
Alleluia, alleluia.

Other songs may be chosen from nos. 225–245, pages **159–161**.

≫ LORD'S PRAYER

103. The celebrant stands in front of the altar and addresses the parents, godparents, and the whole assembly in these or similar words:

Dearly beloved, this child has been reborn in baptism.
He (she) is now called the child of God, for so indeed
he (she) is. In confirmation he (she) will receive the
fullness of God's Spirit. In holy communion he (she)
will share the banquet of Christ's sacrifice, calling God
his (her) Father in the midst of the Church. In the name
of this child, in the Spirit of our common sonship, let us
pray together in the words our Lord has given us:

104. All present join the celebrant in singing or saying:

Our Father,
who art in heaven,
hallowed be thy name;
thy kingdom come;
thy will be done on earth as it is in heaven.
Give us this day our daily bread;
and forgive us our trespasses
as we forgive those who trespass against us;
and lead us not into temptation,
but deliver us from evil.

BLESSING AND DISMISSAL *Raise right hand for God's blessing on parents child* [handwritten]

105. The celebrant first blesses the mother, who holds the child in her arms, then the father, and lastly the entire assembly:

Celebrant:

Mom [handwritten] **God the Father, through his Son, the Virgin Mary's child, has brought joy to all Christian mothers, as they see the hope of eternal life shine on their children. May he bless the mother of this child. She now thanks God for the gift of her child. May she** [*you* handwritten] **be one with him** **(her) in thanking him for ever in heaven, in Christ Jesus our Lord.**

All:

Amen.

Celebrant:

Dad [handwritten] **God is the giver of all life, human and divine. May he bless the father of this child. He and his wife will be the first teachers of their child in the ways of faith. May they be also the best of teachers, bearing witness to the faith by what they** [*you* handwritten] **say and do, in Christ Jesus our Lord.**

All:

Amen.

Hands down [handwritten]

Celebrant:

By God's gift, through water and the Holy Spirit, we are reborn to everlasting life. In his goodness, may he continue to pour out his blessings upon these [*us* handwritten] ~~**sons and daughters of his**~~**. May he make them** [*us* handwritten] **always, wherever they** [*we* handwritten] **may be, faithful members of his holy people. May he send his peace upon all who are gathered here, in Christ Jesus our Lord.**

Gift [handwritten]

All:

Amen.

Celebrant:

May almighty God, the Father, and the Son, ✢ and the Holy Spirit, bless you.

All:

Amen.

Celebrant:

Go in peace.

All:

Thanks be to God.

For other forms of the blessing, see nos. 247–249, pages **162–164**.

106. After the blessing, all may sing a hymn which suitably expresses thanksgiving and Easter joy, or they may sing the song of the Blessed Virgin Mary, the Magnificat.

Where there is the practice of bringing the baptized child to the altar of the Blessed Virgin Mary, this custom is observed if appropriate.

RITE OF BAPTISM
FOR A LARGE NUMBER
OF CHILDREN

CHAPTER III
RITE OF BAPTISM FOR A LARGE NUMBER OF CHILDREN

RECEPTION OF THE CHILDREN

107. The people may sing a psalm or hymn suitable for the occasion. Meanwhile the celebrating priest or deacon, vested in alb or surplice, with a stole (with or without a cope) of festive color, and accompanied by the ministers, goes to the entrance of the church or to that part of the church where the parents and godparents are waiting with those who are to be baptized.

[See no. 34. If there are several priests or deacons present, these may help the celebrant in the parts referred to below.]

108. The celebrant greets all present, and especially the parents and godparents, reminding them briefly of the joy with which the parents welcomed their children as gifts from God, the source of life, who now wishes to bestow his own life on these little ones.

Then the celebrant questions the parents and godparents together:

A Celebrant:

What name do you want to give your children?

Each family answers in turn, giving the names of the children.

Celebrant:

What do you ask of God's Church for these children?

All families together:

Baptism.

But if there is a very large number to be baptized, he omits the first question and asks:

B   **Parents and godparents, what do you ask for these children?**

All families together:
Baptism.

109. The celebrant speaks to the parents in these or similar words:

You have asked to have your children baptized. In doing so you are accepting the responsibility of training them in the practice of the faith. It will be your duty to bring them up to keep God's commandments as Christ taught us, by loving God and our neighbor. Do you clearly understand what you are undertaking?

All parents together:
We do.

110. Then the celebrant turns to the godparents and addresses them in these or similar words:

Are you ready to help these parents in their duty as Christian mothers and fathers?

All the godparents:
We are.

111. The celebrant continues:

My dear children, the Christian community welcomes you with great joy. In its name I claim you for Christ our Savior by the sign of his cross.

He makes the sign of the cross over all the children together, and says:

Parents (or godparents), make the sign of Christ our Savior on the foreheads of your children.

Then the parents (or godparents) sign the children on their foreheads.

[If baptism is to be celebrated at Sunday or weekday Mass, the Order of Mass begins here with the **Lord, have mercy.**]

LITURGY OF THE WORD

SCRIPTURAL READINGS AND HOMILY

112. The celebrant invites the parents, godparents, and the others to take part in the liturgy of the word. Matthew 28:18-20 is read, telling how the apostles were sent to preach the gospel and to baptize:

A reading from the holy Gospel according to Matthew

Go, therefore, and make disciples of all nations, baptizing them in the name of the Father, and of the Son, and of the Holy Spirit.

Jesus said to the Eleven disciples:

"All power in heaven and on earth has been given to me.

Go, therefore, and make disciples of all nations,

> **baptizing them in the name of the Father,**
> **and of the Son, and of the Holy Spirit,**
> **teaching them to observe all that I have commanded**
> > **you.**

And behold, I am with you always, until the end of the
> **age."**

The Gospel of the Lord.

Other passages may also be selected from nos. 44, 186–194, 204–215. See pages **142–150**.

113. After the reading, the celebrant gives a short homily, explaining to those present the significance of what has been read. His purpose will be to lead them to a deeper understanding of the mystery of baptism and to encourage the parents and godparents to a ready acceptance of the responsibilities which arise from the sacrament.

GENERAL INTERCESSIONS

114. Then the general intercessions are said:

Celebrant:

My dear brothers and sisters, let us ask our Lord Jesus Christ to look lovingly on these children who are to be baptized, on their parents and godparents, and on all the baptized.

Leader:

By the mystery of your death and resurrection, bathe these children in light, give them the new life of baptism and welcome them into your holy Church.

All:

Lord, hear our prayer.

Leader:

Through baptism and confirmation, make them your faithful followers and witnesses to your gospel.

All:

Lord, hear our prayer.

Leader:

Lead them by a holy life to the joys of God's kingdom.

All:

Lord, hear our prayer.

Leader:

Make the lives of their parents and godparents examples of faith to inspire these children.

All:

Lord, hear our prayer.

Leader:

Keep their families always in your love.

All:

Lord, hear our prayer.

Leader:

Renew the grace of our baptism in each one of us.

All:

Lord, hear our prayer.

Other forms may be chosen from nos. 217–220, pages **151–154**. The invocation of the saints (see no. 48, page **28**) may be omitted.

PRAYER OF EXORCISM

115. The prayer of the faithful is concluded with the prayer of exorcism:

Almighty and ever-living God,

you sent your only Son into the world

to cast out the power of Satan, spirit of evil,

to rescue man from the kingdom of darkness,

and bring him into the splendor of your kingdom of light.

We pray for these children:

set them free from original sin,

make them temples of your glory,

and send your Holy Spirit to dwell within them.

(We ask this) through Christ our Lord.

All:

Amen.

For another form of the prayer of exorcism, see no. 221, page **155**.

Because of the large number of children to be baptized, the celebrant does not anoint them with oil of catechumens. He imposes his hands over all the children at once and says:

May you have strength in the power of Christ our Savior, who lives and reigns for ever and ever.

All:

Amen.

116. Then they go to the place where baptism is celebrated.

CELEBRATION OF THE SACRAMENT

117. When they come to the font, the celebrant briefly reminds the congregation of the wonderful work of God whose plan it is to sanctify man, body and soul, through water. He may use these or similar words:

My dear brothers and sisters, God uses the sacrament of water to give his divine life to those who believe in him.

Let us turn to him in our faith, and ask him to pour his gift of life from this font on the children he has chosen.

BLESSING AND INVOCATION OF GOD OVER BAPTISMAL WATER

118. Then, turning to the font, he says the following blessing:

Celebrant:

Merciful Father, from the font of baptism you have given us new life as your sons and daughters.

All:

Blessed be God (or some other suitable acclamation by the people).

Celebrant:

You bring together all who are baptized in water and the Holy Spirit to be one people in Jesus Christ your Son.

All:

Blessed be God.

Celebrant:

You have made us free by pouring the Spirit of your love into our hearts, so that we will enjoy your peace.

All:

Blessed be God.

Celebrant:

You have chosen your baptized people to announce with joy the Good News of Christ to all nations.

All:

Blessed be God.

A   Celebrant:

Come and ✠ bless this water in which your servants are to be baptized. You have called them to the washing of new life in the faith of your Church, so that they may have eternal life. We ask this through Christ our Lord.

All:

Amen.

119. During the Easter season, if there is baptismal water already blessed, the celebrant omits the last part of the blessing **Come and bless**, and concludes in this way:

B   **By the mystery of this consecrated water, you bring your servants to spiritual rebirth. You have called them to the washing of new life in the faith of your Church, so that they may have eternal life. We ask this through Christ our Lord.**

All:

Amen.

Other forms may be chosen from nos. 223–224, pages **156–158**.

RENUNCIATION OF SIN AND PROFESSION OF FAITH

120. The celebrant speaks to the parents and godparents in these words:

Dear parents and godparents: You have come here to present these children for baptism. By water and the Holy Spirit they are to receive the gift of new life from God, who is love.

On your part, you must make it your constant care to bring them up in the practice of the faith. See that the divine life which God gives them is kept safe from the poison of sin, to grow always stronger in their hearts.

If your faith makes you ready to accept this responsibility, renew now the vows of your baptism. Reject sin; profess your faith in Christ Jesus. This is the faith of the Church. This is the faith in which these children are about to be baptized.

121. The celebrant questions the parents and godparents.

A   Celebrant:

Do you reject Satan?

Parents and godparents:

I do.

Celebrant:

And all his works?

Parents and godparents:

I do.

Celebrant:

And all his empty promises?

Parents and godparents:

I do.

or:

B   Celebrant:

Do you reject sin, so as to live in the freedom of God's children?

Parents and godparents:

I do.

Celebrant:

Do you reject the glamor of evil, and refuse to be mastered by sin?

Parents and godparents:

I do.

Celebrant:

Do you reject Satan, father of sin and prince of darkness?

Parents and godparents:

I do.

According to circumstances this second form may be expressed with greater precision by the conferences of bishops, especially in places where it is necessary for the parents and godparents to reject superstitious and magical practices used with children.

122. Next the celebrant asks for the threefold profession of faith from the parents and godparents:

Celebrant:

Do you believe in God, the Father almighty, creator of heaven and earth?

Parents and godparents:

I do.

Celebrant:

Do you believe in Jesus Christ, his only Son, our Lord, who was born of the Virgin Mary, was crucified, died, and was buried, rose from the dead, and is now seated at the right hand of the Father?

Parents and godparents:

I do.

Celebrant:

Do you believe in the Holy Spirit, the holy catholic Church, the communion of saints, the forgiveness of sins, the resurrection of the body, and life everlasting?

Parents and godparents:

I do.

[If the baptism is celebrated during the Easter Vigil, the rite continues with no. 124 below.]

123. The celebrant and the congregation give their assent to this profession of faith:

Celebrant:

This is our faith. This is the faith of the Church. We are proud to profess it, in Christ Jesus our Lord.

All:

Amen.

If desired, some other formula may be used instead, or a suitable song by which the community expresses its faith with a single voice.

BAPTISM

124. If there are several ministers because of the large number to be baptized, each of them questions the parents and godparents, using the name of the individual child:

Celebrant:

Is it your will that N. should be baptized in the faith of the Church, which we have all professed with you?

Parents and godparents:

It is.

He baptizes the child, saying:

N., I baptize you in the name of the Father,

He immerses the child or pours water upon it.

and of the Son,

He immerses the child or pours water upon it a second time.

and of the Holy Spirit.

He immerses the child or pours water upon it a third time.

He asks the same question and performs the same action for each child.

If the baptism is performed by the pouring of water, it is preferable that the child be held by the mother (or father). Where, however, it is felt that the existing custom should be retained, the godmother (or godfather) may hold the child. If baptism is by immersion, the mother or father (godmother or godfather) lifts the child out of the font.

While the children are being baptized, the community can make acclamations or sing hymns (see nos. 225–245, pages 159–161). Some passages from Scripture may also be read, or a sacred silence observed.

EXPLANATORY RITES

ANOINTING AFTER BAPTISM

125. Then the celebrant says the formula of anointing once for all the children:

God the Father of our Lord Jesus Christ has freed you from sin, given you a new birth by water and the Holy Spirit, and welcomed you into his holy people. He now anoints you with the chrism of salvation. As Christ was anointed Priest, Prophet, and King, so may you live always as members of his body, sharing everlasting life.

All:

Amen.

Then the ministers anoint each child on the crown of the head with the sacred chrism, in silence. But if the number of children is extremely large, the conferences of bishops may decide that the anointing with chrism may be omitted. [In the United States the anointing may not be omitted.] In this case, an adapted formula is used:

God the Father of our Lord Jesus Christ has freed you from sin, and has given you a new birth by water and the Holy Spirit. He has made you Christians now, and has welcomed you into his holy people. As Christ was anointed Priest, Prophet, and King, so may you live always as members of his body, sharing everlasting life.

All:

Amen.

CLOTHING WITH WHITE GARMENT

126. The celebrant says:

My dear children, you have become a new creation, and have clothed yourselves in Christ.

See in this white garment the outward sign of your Christian dignity. With your family and friends to help you by word and example, bring that dignity unstained into the everlasting life of heaven.

All:

Amen.

The white garments are put on the children. A different color is not permitted unless demanded by local custom. It is desirable that the families provide the garments.

[If baptism is celebrated during the Easter Vigil, the rite of baptism ends here, and the rite of the Easter Vigil continues.]

LIGHTED CANDLE

127. The celebrant takes the paschal candle and says:

Receive the light of Christ. Parents and godparents, this light is entrusted to you to be kept burning brightly. These children of yours have been enlightened by Christ. They are to walk always as children of the light. May they keep the flame of faith alive in their hearts.

**When the Lord comes, may they go out to meet him
with all the saints in the heavenly kingdom.**

Candles are distributed to the families. The head of one family
lights his candle from the Easter candle and passes the flame
on to the rest. Meanwhile the community sings a baptismal
song, such as:

**You have put on Christ,
in him you have been baptized.
Alleluia, alleluia.**

Other hymns may be chosen from nos. 225–245, pages **159–161**.

Meanwhile, unless the baptisms were performed in the sanctuary, there is a procession to the altar. The lighted candles are
carried for the children.

[If baptism is celebrated during Sunday or weekday Mass, the
Mass continues in the usual way with the offertory.]

CONCLUSION OF THE RITE

LORD'S PRAYER

128. The celebrant stands in front of the altar and addresses
the parents, godparents, and the whole assembly in these or
similar words:

**Dearly beloved, these children have been reborn in
baptism. They are now called children of God, for so
indeed they are. In confirmation they will receive the
fullness of God's Spirit. In holy communion they will
share the banquet of Christ's sacrifice, calling God their
Father in the midst of the Church. In their name, in the
Spirit of our common sonship, let us pray together in
the words our Lord has given us:**

129. All present join the celebrant in singing or saying:

Our Father,
who art in heaven,
hallowed be thy name;
thy kingdom come;
thy will be done on earth as it is in heaven.
Give us this day our daily bread;
and forgive us our trespasses
as we forgive those who trespass against us;
and lead us not into temptation,
but deliver us from evil.

BLESSING AND DISMISSAL

130. The celebrant blesses the entire assembly, and dismisses them:

My brothers and sisters, we commend you to the mercy and grace of God our almighty Father, of his only Son, and of the Holy Spirit. May he protect your paths, so that walking in the light of faith, you may come to the good things he has promised us.

May almighty God, the Father, and the Son, ✝ and the Holy Spirit bless you.

All:

Amen.

Celebrant:

Go in peace.

All:

Thanks be to God.

For other forms of the blessing, see nos. 70, 247–248, pages **45,** **162–163**.

131. After the blessing, all may sing a hymn which suitably expresses thanksgiving and Easter joy, or they may sing the song of the Blessed Virgin Mary, the Magnificat.

RITE OF BAPTISM
FOR CHILDREN
ADMINISTERED BY A CATECHIST
WHEN NO PRIEST OR DEACON
IS AVAILABLE

CHAPTER IV
RITE OF BAPTISM FOR CHILDREN ADMINISTERED BY A CATECHIST WHEN NO PRIEST OR DEACON IS AVAILABLE

RECEPTION OF THE CHILDREN

132. While the faithful sing a suitable psalm or hymn, the catechist and the ministers approach the door of the church or the part of the church where the parents, godparents, and the children to be baptized are waiting.

If there is a large group of persons to be baptized, the catechist may be assisted by others in the act of baptism, as noted below.

133. The catechist greets all present, and especially the parents and godparents, reminding them briefly of the joy with which the parents welcomed their children as gifts from God, the source of life, who now wishes to bestow his own life on these little ones.

Then he questions the parents and godparents together in these or similar words:

A **What name do you give your children?** (or: **have you given?**)

Each family answers in turn, giving the names of the children.

Catechist:

What do you ask of God's Church for these children?

All families together:

Baptism.

If there are many children to be baptized, the first question is omitted and the catechist asks:

B Parents and godparents, what do you ask for these children?

All families together:

Baptism.

134. Then the catechist speaks to the parents:

Parents, you have asked to have your children baptized. In doing so you are accepting the responsibility of training them in the practice of the faith. It will be your duty to bring them up to keep God's commandments as Christ taught us, by loving God and our neighbor. Do you clearly understand what you are undertaking?

All parents together:

We do.

135. Then turning to the godparents, the catechist asks:

Godparents, are you ready to help these parents in their duty as Christian mothers and fathers?

All the godparents together:

We do.

136. The catechist continues:

My dear children, the Christian community welcomes you with great joy. In its name I claim you for Christ our Savior by the sign of his cross.

He makes the sign of the cross over all the children together, and says:

Parents (or godparents), make the sign of Christ our Savior on the foreheads of your children.

Then the parents (or godparents) sign the children on their foreheads.

LITURGY OF THE WORD

READING AND HOMILY OR SHORT TALK

137. The catechist invites the parents, godparents, and the others to take part in the liturgy of the word. Matthew 28:18-20 is read, telling how the apostles were sent to preach the gospel and to baptize:

A reading from the holy Gospel according to Matthew

Go, therefore, and make disciples of all nations, baptizing them in the name of the Father, and of the Son, and of the Holy Spirit.

Jesus said to the Eleven disciples:
"All power in heaven and on earth has been given to me.
Go, therefore, and make disciples of all nations,
  baptizing them in the name of the Father,
  and of the Son, and of the Holy Spirit,
  teaching them to observe all that I have commanded
    you.
And behold, I am with you always, until the end of
  the age."

The Gospel of the Lord.

Other passages may also be selected from nos. 186–194, 204–215, pages **142–150**. If songs and hymns are sung, see nos. 195–203, pages **138–142**. After the reading, the catechist can give a brief homily in the way determined by the bishop.

138. In the place of the scripture reading and the homily, the catechist can, if necessary, gives this talk:

In baptism, Christ will come to meet these children. He entrusted this sacrament to his Church when he sent forth his apostles with these words: "Go, make disciples of all nations, and baptize them in the name of the Father, and of the Son, and of the Holy Spirit."

As you know, these children will be given countless gifts in this great sacrament: they will be freed from sin; they will become members of the Church; they will become God's own children. But since man is unable to accomplish such wonders, we must pray together with humility and faith for these blessings.

May God our Father see in the fellowship of our community the faith of his Church, and hear in our prayer the voice of Jesus his Son. As he promised us through Christ, may he bless these children by the power of his Holy Spirit.

GENERAL INTERCESSIONS

139. Then the general intercessions are said:

Catechist:

My dear brothers and sisters, let us ask our Lord Jesus Christ to look lovingly on these children who are to be baptized, on their parents and godparents, and on all the baptized.

Leader:

By the mystery of your death and resurrection, bathe these children in light, give them the new life of baptism and welcome them into your holy Church.

All:

Lord, hear our prayer.

Leader:

Through baptism and confirmation, make them your faithful followers and witnesses to your gospel.

All:

Lord, hear our prayer.

Leader:

Lead them by a holy life to the joys of God's kingdom.

All:

Lord, hear our prayer.

Leader:

Make the lives of their parents and godparents examples of faith to inspire these children.

All:

Lord, hear our prayer.

Leader:

Keep their families always in your love.

All:

Lord, hear our prayer.

Leader:

Renew the grace of our baptism in each one of us.

All:

Lord, hear our prayer.

Other forms may be chosen from nos. 217–220, pages **151–154**.

Then the catechist invites all present to invoke the saints:

Holy Mary, Mother of God,   pray for us.
Saint John the Baptist,   pray for us.
Saint Joseph,   pray for us.
Saint Peter and Saint Paul,   pray for us.

The names of other saints may be added, especially the patrons of the children to be baptized, and of the church or locality. The litany concludes:

All holy men and women,   pray for us.

140. The prayer of exorcism and the anointing with oil of catechumens are omitted.

CELEBRATION OF THE SACRAMENT

BLESSING AND INVOCATION OF GOD OVER BAPTISMAL WATER

141. With the parents and godparents carrying the children who are to be baptized, the catechist comes to the font. He invites all to pray:

My dear brothers and sisters, let us ask God to give these children new life in abundance through water and the Holy Spirit.

142. If there is no blessed water available, the catechist stands before the font and says this invocation:

A   Catechist:

Merciful Father, from the font of baptism you have given us new life as your sons and daughters.

All:

Blessed be God (or some other suitable acclamation by the people).

Catechist:

You bring together all who are baptized in water and the Holy Spirit to be one people in Jesus Christ your Son.

All:

Blessed be God.

Catechist:

You have made us free by pouring the Spirit of your love into our hearts, so that we will enjoy your peace.

All:

Blessed be God.

Catechist:

You have chosen your baptized people to announce with joy the Good News of Christ to all nations.

All:

Blessed be God.

Catechist:

Come and bless this water in which your servants are to be baptized. You have called them to the washing of new life in the faith of your Church, so that they may have eternal life. We ask this through Christ our Lord.

All:

Amen.

143. If blessed water is available, he says the following invocation:

B **Father of our Lord Jesus Christ,**
source of all life and love,
you are glorified throughout the world
by the simple joys and daily cares
of mothers and fathers.

In the beauty of a child's birth
and in the mystery of his rebirth to eternal life,
you give us a glimpse of all creation:
it is guided by your fatherly love,
unfolding in fruitfulness to perfection
in Jesus Christ your Son.

In your kindness
hear the prayers of the Church and of these parents.
Look upon these children with love,
and keep them from the power of sin.
Since they are a gift from you, Father,
welcome them into the kingdom of your Son.

You have created this water,
and made it clean, refreshing, and life-giving.
You have made it holy through the baptism of Christ,
that by the power of the Holy Spirit
it may give your people a new birth.

**When these children are baptized into the mystery
of Christ's suffering, death, and resurrection,
may they be worthy to become members of your Church,
your very own children.
Father, may they rejoice
with Jesus your Son and the Holy Spirit
for ever and ever.**

All:
Amen.

RENUNCIATION OF SIN AND PROFESSION OF FAITH

144. The catechist speaks to the parents and godparents in these words:

Dear parents and godparents: You have come here to present these children for baptism. By water and the Holy Spirit, they are to receive the gift of new life from God, who is love.

On your part, you must make it your constant care to bring them up in the practice of the faith. See that the divine life which God gives them is kept safe from the poison of sin, to grow always stronger in their hearts.

If your faith makes you ready to accept this responsibility, renew now the vows of your baptism. Reject sin; profess your faith in Christ Jesus. This is the faith of the Church. This is the faith in which these children are about to be baptized.

145. Then he asks them:

A   Catechist:
Do you reject Satan?

Parents and godparents:
I do.

Catechist:

And all his works?

Parents and godparents:
I do.

Catechist:

And all his empty promises?

Parents and godparents:
I do.

B   Catechist:

Do you reject sin, so as to live in the freedom of God's children?

Parents and godparents:
I do.

Catechist:

Do you reject the glamor of evil, and refuse to be mastered by sin?

Parents and godparents:
I do.

Catechist:

Do you reject Satan, father of sin and prince of darkness?

Parents and godparents:
I do.

According to circumstances this second form may be expressed with greater precision by the conference of bishops, especially in places where it is necessary for the parents and godparents to reject superstitious and magical practices used with children.

146. Then the catechist asks for the threefold profession of faith from the parents and godparents:

Catechist:

Do you believe in God, the Father almighty, creator of heaven and earth?

Parents and godparents:

I do.

Catechist:

Do you believe in Jesus Christ, his only Son, our Lord, who was born of the Virgin Mary, was crucified, died, and was buried, rose from the dead, and is now seated at the right hand of the Father?

Parents and godparents:

I do.

Catechist:

Do you believe in the Holy Spirit, the holy catholic Church, the communion of saints, the forgiveness of sins, the resurrection of the body, and life everlasting?

Parents and godparents:

I do.

147. The catechist and the congregation give their assent to this profession of faith:

Catechist:

This is our faith. This is the faith of the Church. We are proud to profess it, in Christ Jesus our Lord.

All:

Amen.

If desired, some other formula may be used instead, or a suitable song by which the community expresses its faith with a single voice.

BAPTISM

148. The catechist invites the first of the families to approach the font. Using the name of the individual child, he asks the parents and godparents:

Is it your will that N. should be baptized in the faith of the Church, which we have all professed with you?

Parents and godparents:
It is.

He baptizes the child, saying:

N., I baptize you in the name of the Father,

He immerses the child or pours water upon it.

and of the Son,

He immerses the child or pours water upon it a second time.

and of the Holy Spirit.

He immerses the child or pours water upon it a third time.

If baptism is performed by the pouring of water, it is preferable that the child be held by the mother or father. Where, however, it is felt that the existing custom should be retained, the godmother or godfather may hold the child. If baptism is by immersion, the parent or godparent lifts the child out of the font.

149. If the number of children to be baptized is large, and other catechists are present, these may baptize some of the children in the way described above, and with the same form (no. 148).

150. While the children are being baptized, the community can make acclamations or sing hymns (see nos. 225–245, pages **159–161**). Some passages from scripture may also be read, or a sacred silence observed.

151. The anointing with the chrism is omitted. The catechist says once for all the newly-baptized children:

God the Father of our Lord Jesus Christ has freed you from sin, and has given you a new birth by water and the Holy Spirit. He has made you Christians now, and has welcomed you into his holy people. As Christ was anointed Priest, Prophet, and King, so may you live always as members of his body, sharing everlasting life.

All:

Amen.

CLOTHING WITH WHITE GARMENT

152. The catechist says:

My dear children, you have become a new creation, and have clothed yourselves in Christ.

See in this white garment the outward sign of your Christian dignity. With your family and friends to help you by word and example, bring that dignity unstained into the everlasting life of heaven.

All:

Amen.

The white garments are put on the children. A different color is not permitted unless demanded by local custom. It is desirable that the families provide the garments.

LIGHTED CANDLE

153. The catechist takes the Easter candle and says:

Receive the light of Christ. Parents and godparents, this light is entrusted to you to be kept burning brightly. These children of yours have been enlightened by Christ. They are to walk always as children of the light. May they keep the flame of faith alive in their hearts.

When the Lord comes, may they go out to meet him with all the saints in the heavenly kingdom.

Candles are distributed to the families. The head of one family lights his candle from the Easter candle and passes the flame on to the rest. Meanwhile the community sings a baptismal song, such as:

**You have put on Christ,
in him you have been baptized.
Alleluia, alleluia.**

Other hymns may be chosen from nos. 225–245, pages **159–161**.

Meanwhile, unless the baptisms were performed in the sanctuary, there is a procession to the altar. The lighted candles are carried for the children.

CONCLUSION OF THE RITE

LORD'S PRAYER

154. The catechist stands in front of the altar and addresses the parents, godparents, and the whole assembly in these or similar words:

Dearly beloved, these children have been reborn in baptism. They are now called children of God, for so indeed they are. In confirmation they will receive the fullness of God's Spirit. In holy communion they will share the banquet of Christ's sacrifice, calling God their Father in the midst of the Church. In their name, in the spirit of common sonship, let us pray together in the words our Lord has given us:

155. All say together:

**Our Father,
who art in heaven,
hallowed be thy name;
thy kingdom come;
thy will be done on earth as it is in heaven.
Give us this day our daily bread;
and forgive us our trespasses
as we forgive those who trespass against us;
and lead us not into temptation,
but deliver us from evil.**

Blessing and Dismissal

The catechist invokes the blessing of God and dismisses those present, saying:

My brothers and sisters, we commend you to the mercy and grace of God our almighty Father, of his only Son, and of the Holy Spirit. May he protect your paths, so that walking in the light of faith, you may come to the good things he has promised us.

All:

Amen.

Catechist:

Go in peace.

All:

Thanks be to God.

156. After the blessing, all may sing a hymn which suitably expresses thanksgiving and Easter joy, or they may sing the song of the Blessed Virgin Mary, the Magnificat.

RITE OF BAPTISM
FOR CHILDREN
IN DANGER OF DEATH
WHEN NO PRIEST
OR DEACON IS AVAILABLE

CHAPTER V
RITE OF BAPTISM FOR CHILDREN IN DANGER OF DEATH WHEN NO PRIEST OR DEACON IS AVAILABLE

157. Water, even though not blessed, is prepared for the rite. The parents, godparents, and if possible. some friends and neighbors of the family gather around the sick child. The minister, who is any suitable member of the Church, begins with this brief prayer of the faithful:

Let us ask almighty God to look with mercy on this child who is about to receive the grace of baptism, on his (her) parents and godparents, and on all baptized persons.

Through baptism, welcome this child into your Church.
R⁊. Lord, hear our prayer.

Through baptism, make him (her) one of your adopted children.
R⁊. Lord, hear our prayer.

Through baptism, he (she) is being buried in the likeness of Christ's death. May he (she) also share in the glory of his resurrection.
R⁊. Lord, hear our prayer.

Renew the grace of our baptism in each one of us.
R⁊. Lord, hear our prayer.

May all the followers of Christ, baptized into one body, always live united in faith and love.
R⁊. Lord, hear our prayer.

158. The prayer of the faithful concludes with this prayer:

Father of our Lord Jesus Christ,
source of all life and love,
you know the anxiety of parents
and you lighten their burden
by your fatherly care for all children in danger.
You reveal the depth of your love
by offering them a new and eternal birth.

In your kindness, hear our prayers:
keep this child from the power of sin,
and welcome him (her) with love
    into the kingdom of your Son.

By water and by the power of the Holy Spirit,
may this child, whom we now call N.,
share in the mystery of Christ's death
so that he (she) may also share
    in the mystery of Christ's resurrection.

May he (she) become your adopted son (daughter),
and share the inheritance of Christ.
Grant that he (she) may rejoice
    in the fellowship of your Church
with your only Son and the Holy Spirit
for ever and ever.
R̽. Amen.

159. Then they make the profession of faith. The minister says
to all present:

A **Let us remember our own baptism, and profess our**
   faith in Jesus Christ. This is the faith of the Church, the
   faith into which children are baptized.

   Then he asks:

   Do you believe in God, the Father almighty, creator of
   heaven and earth?
   R̽. I do.

Minister:

Do you believe in Jesus Christ, his only Son, our Lord, who was born of the Virgin Mary, was crucified, died, and was buried, rose from the dead, and is now seated at the right hand of the Father?
℞. I do.

Minister:

Do you believe in the Holy Spirit, the holy catholic Church, the communion of saints, the forgiveness of sins, the resurrection of the body, and life everlasting?
℞. I do.

The profession of faith may also be made, if desirable, by reciting the Apostles' Creed:

B **I believe in God, the Father almighty,**
Creator of heaven and earth;
and in Jesus Christ, his only Son, our Lord,
who was conceived by the Holy Spirit,
born of the Virgin Mary,
suffered under Pontius Pilate,
was crucified, died, and was buried.
He descended into hell;
the third day he rose again from the dead;
he ascended into heaven,
sitteth at the right hand of God, the Father almighty,
from thence he shall come to judge the living and
the dead.
I believe in the Holy Spirit,
the holy Catholic Church,
the communion of saints,
the forgiveness of sins,
the resurrection of the body,
and life everlasting. Amen.

160. Then the minister baptizes the child, saying:

N., I baptize you in the name of the Father,

He pours water upon the child.

and of the Son,

He pours water upon the child a second time.

and of the Holy Spirit.

He pours water upon the child a third time.

161. Omitting all other ceremonies, he may give the white garment to the child. The minister says:

N., you have become a new creation, and have clothed yourself in Christ.

See in this white garment the outward sign of your Christian dignity. May you bring it unstained into the everlasting life of heaven.

162. The celebration concludes with the recitation of the Lord's Prayer:

Our Father,
who art in heaven,
hallowed be thy name;
thy kingdom come;
thy will be done on earth as it is in heaven.
Give us this day our daily bread;
and forgive us our trespasses
as we forgive those who trespass against us;
and lead us not into temptation,
but deliver us from evil.

163. If no one there is capable of directing the prayer, any member of the Church may baptize, after reciting the Apostles' Creed, by pouring water on the child while reciting the customary words (see no. 160, above). The creed may be omitted if necessary.

164. At the moment of death, it is sufficient for the minister to omit all other ceremonies and pour water on the child while saying the usual words (see no. 160, above). It is desirable that the minister, as far as possible, should use one or two witnesses.

RITE OF BRINGING
A BAPTIZED CHILD
TO THE CHURCH

CHAPTER VI
RITE OF BRINGING A BAPTIZED CHILD TO THE CHURCH

RECEPTION OF THE CHILD

165. The people may sing a psalm or song suitable for the occasion. Meanwhile the celebrating priest or deacon, vested in alb or surplice, with a stole (with or without a cope) of festive color, and accompanied by the ministers, goes to the entrance of the church where the parents and godparents are waiting with the child.

166. The celebrant greets all present, and especially the parents and godparents. He praises them for having had the child baptized without delay, and thanks God and congratulates the parents on the child's return to health.

167. First the celebrant questions the parents:

Celebrant:

What name have you given your child?

Parents:

N.

Celebrant:

What do you ask of God's Church, now that your child has been baptized?

Parents:

We ask that the whole community will know that he (she) has been received into the Church.

The first reply may be given by someone other than the parents if local custom gives him the right to name the child.

In the second response the parents may use other words, such as **that he (she) is a Christian** or **that he (she) has been baptized.**

168. Then the celebrant speaks to the parents in these or similar words:

Celebrant:

Do you realize that in bringing your child to the Church, you are accepting the duty of raising him (her) in the faith, so that by observing the commandments he (she) will love God and neighbor as Christ taught us?

Parents:

We do.

169. Then the celebrant turns to the godparents and addresses them in these or similar words:

Are you ready to help the mother and father of this child to carry out their duty as Christian parents?

Godparents:

We are.

170. The celebrant continues:

N., the Christian community welcomes you with great joy, now that you have recovered your health. We now bear witness that you have been received as a member of the Church. In the name of the community I sign you with the cross of Christ, who gave you a new life in baptism and made you a member of his Church. I invite your parents (and godparents) to do the same.

He signs the child on the forehead in silence. Then he invites the parents and (if it seems appropriate) the godparents to do the same.

171. The celebrant invites the parents, godparents, and all who are present to take part in the liturgy of the word. If circumstances permit, there is a procession to the place where this will be celebrated, during which a song is sung, such as Psalm 84:7, 8, 9ab:

Will you not give us life;
**   and shall not your people rejoice in you?**
Show us, O Lord, your kindness,

and grant us your salvation.
I will hear what God proclaims;
the Lord—for he proclaims peace to his people.

LITURGY OF THE WORD

SCRIPTURAL READINGS AND HOMILY

172. One or even two of the following gospel passages are read, during which all may sit if convenient.

1   John 3:1-6

A reading from the holy Gospel according to John
No one can see the Kingdom of God without being born from above.

**There was a Pharisee named Nicodemus, a ruler of
the Jews.
He came to Jesus at night and said to him,
"Rabbi, we know that you are a teacher who has
come from God,
for no one can do these signs that you are doing
unless God is with him."
Jesus answered and said to him,
"Amen, amen, I say to you,
unless one is born from above,
he cannot see the Kingdom of God."
Nicodemus said to him,
"How can a man once grown old be born again?
Surely he cannot reenter his mother's womb and be
born again, can he?"
Jesus answered,
"Amen, amen, I say to you,
unless one is born of water and Spirit
he cannot enter the Kingdom of God.
What is born of flesh is flesh
and what is born of spirit is spirit."
The Gospel of the Lord.**

2   Matthew 28:18-20

A reading from the holy Gospel according to Matthew

Go, therefore, and make disciples of all nations, baptizing them in the name of the Father, and of the Son, and of the Holy Spirit.

Jesus said to the Eleven disciples:

"All power in heaven and on earth has been given to me.

Go, therefore, and make disciples of all nations,
> **baptizing them in the name of the Father,**
> **and of the Son, and of the Holy Spirit,**
> **teaching them to observe all that I have commanded**
>> **you.**

And behold, I am with you always, until the end of
> **the age."**

The Gospel of the Lord.

3   Mark 1:9-11

A reading from the holy Gospel according to Mark

Jesus was baptized in the Jordan by John.

Jesus came from Nazareth of Galilee
> **and was baptized in the Jordan by John.**

On coming up out of the water he saw the heavens
> **being torn open**
> **and the Spirit, like a dove, descending upon him.**

And a voice came from the heavens,
> **"You are my beloved Son; with you I am well**
>> **pleased."**

The Gospel of the Lord.

4   Mark 10:13-16

A reading from the holy Gospel according to Mark

Let the children come to me; do not prevent them.

People were bringing children to Jesus that he might
        touch them,
    but the disciples rebuked them.
When Jesus saw this he became indignant and said
        to them,
    "Let the children come to me; do not prevent them,
    for the Kingdom of God belongs to such as these.
Amen, I say to you,
    whoever does not accept the Kingdom of God like
        a child
    will not enter it."
Then he embraced them and blessed them,
    placing his hands on them.

The Gospel of the Lord.

The passages listed in nos. 186–194 and 204–215 may also be chosen (see pages 131–137 and 142–150), or other passages which better meet the wishes or needs of the parents, such as the following:

1   1 Kings 17:17-24

A reading from the first Book of Kings

Some time later the son of the mistress of the house fell sick, and his sickness grew more severe until he stopped breathing. So she said to Elijah, "Why have you done this to me, O man of God? Have you come to me to call attention to my guilt and to kill my son?" "Give me your son," Elijah said to her. Taking him from her lap, he carried him to the upper room where he was staying, and laid him on his own bed. He called out to the LORD: "O LORD, my God, will you afflict even the widow with whom I am staying by killing her son?" Then he stretched himself out upon the child three times and called out to the LORD: "O LORD, my God, let the life breath return to the body of this child." The LORD heard the prayer of Elijah; the life breath returned to the child's body and he revived. Taking the child, Elijah brought him down into the house from the upper room and gave him to his mother. "See!" Elijah said to her, "your son is alive." "Now indeed I know that you are a man of God," the woman replied to Elijah. "The word of the LORD comes truly from your mouth."

The word of the Lord.

2

A reading from the second Book of Kings

One day Elisha came to Shunem, where there was a woman of influence, who urged him to dine with her. Afterward, whenever he passed by, he used to stop there to dine. So she said to her husband, "I know that he is a holy man of God. Since he visits us often, let us arrange a little room on the roof and furnish it for him with a bed, table, chair, and lamp, so that when he comes to us he can stay there." Some time later Elisha arrived and stayed in the room overnight. Then he said to his servant Gehazi, "Call this Shunammite woman." He did so, and when she stood before Elisha, he told Gehazi, "Say to her, 'You have lavished all this care on us; what can we do for you? Can we say a good word for you to the king or to the commander of the army?'" She replied, "I am living among my own people." Later Elisha asked, "Can something be done for her?" "Yes!" Gehazi answered. "She has no son, and her husband is getting on in years." "Call her," said Elisha. When she had been called, and stood at the door, Elisha promised, "This time next year you will be fondling a baby son." "Please, my lord," she protested, "you are a man of God; do not deceive your servant." Yet the woman conceived, and by the same time the following year she had given birth to a son, as Elisha promised.

The day came when the child was old enough to go out to his father among the reapers. "My head hurts!" he complained to his father. "Carry him to his mother," the father said to a servant. The servant picked him up and carried him to his mother; he stayed with her until noon, when he died in her lap. The mother took him upstairs and laid him on the bed of the man of God.

Closing the door on him, she went out and called to her husband, "Let me have a servant and a donkey. I must go quickly to the man of God, and I will be back." "Why are you going to him today?" he asked. "It is neither the new moon nor the sabbath." But she bade him good-bye, and when the donkey was saddled, said to her servant: "Lead on! Do not stop my donkey unless I tell you to." She kept going till she reached the man of God on Mount Carmel. When he spied her at a distance, the man of God said to his servant Gehazi: There is the Shunammite! Hurry to meet her, and ask if all is well with her, with her husband, and with the boy." "Greetings," she replied. But when she reached the man of God on the mountain, she clasped his feet. Gehazi came near to push her away, but the man of God said: "Let her alone, she is in bitter anguish; the Lord hid it from me and did not let me know." "Did I ask my lord for a son?" she cried out. "Did I not beg you not to deceive me?" "Gird your loins," Elisha said to Gehazi, "take my staff with you and be off; if you meet anyone, do not greet him, and if anyone greets you, do not answer. Lay my staff upon the boy." But the boy's mother cried out: "As the Lord lives and as you yourself live, I will not release you." So he started to go back with her.

Meanwhile, Gehazi had gone on ahead and had laid the staff upon the boy, but there was no sound or sign of life. He returned to meet Elisha and informed him that the boy had not awakened. When Elisha reached the house, he found the boy lying dead. He went in, closed the door on them both, and prayed to the Lord. Then he lay upon the child on the bed, placing his mouth upon the child's mouth, his eyes upon the eyes, and his hands upon the

hands. As Elisha stretched himself over the child, the body became warm. He arose, paced up and down the room, and then once more lay down upon the boy, who now sneezed seven times and opened his eyes. Elisha summoned Gehazi and said, "Call the Shunammite." She came at his call, and Elisha said to her, "Take your son." She came in and fell at his feet in gratitude; then she took her son and left the room.

The word of the Lord.

> Between the readings, responsorial psalms or verses may be sung, as given in nos. 195–203, pages **138–142**.

173. After the reading, the celebrant gives a brief homily, explaining to those present the significance of what has been read. His purpose will be to lead them to a deeper understanding of the mystery of baptism and to encourage parents and godparents to a ready acceptance of the responsibilities which arise from the sacrament.

174. After the homily, or in the course of or after the litany, it is desirable to have a period of silence while all pray at the invitation of the celebrant. A suitable hymn may follow, such as one chosen from nos. 225–245, pages **159–161**.

GENERAL INTERCESSIONS

175. Then the general intercessions are said:

Celebrant:

Let us ask our Lord Jesus Christ to look lovingly on this child, on his (her) parents and godparents, and on all the baptized.

Leader:

May this child always show gratitude to God for his (her) baptism and recovery.

All:

Lord, hear our prayer.

Leader:

Help him (her) always to be a living member of your Church.

All:

Lord, hear our prayer.

Leader:

Inspire him (her) to hear, follow, and witness to your gospel.

All:

Lord, hear our prayer.

Leader:

May he (she) come with joy to the table of your sacrifice.

All:

Lord, hear our prayer.

Leader:

Help him (her) to love God and neighbor as you have taught us.

All:

Lord, hear our prayer.

Leader:

May he (she) grow in holiness and wisdom by listening to his (her) fellow Christians and following their example.

All:

Lord, hear our prayer.

Leader:

Keep all your followers united in faith and love for ever.

All:

Lord, hear our prayer.

176. The celebrant next invites all present to invoke the saints:

Holy Mary, Mother of God,   pray for us.
Saint John the Baptist,   pray for us.
Saint Joseph,   pray for us.
Saint Peter and Saint Paul,   pray for us.

The names of other saints may be added, especially the patrons of the child and of the church or locality. The litany concludes:

All holy men and women,   pray for us.

177. Then the celebrant says:

Father of our Lord Jesus Christ,
source of all life and love,
you are glorified by the loving care these parents
have shown this child.
You rescue children from danger and save them
in baptism.

Your Church thanks you and prays for your child N.
You have brought him (her) out of the kingdom
of darkness
and into your marvelous light.
You have made him (her) your adopted child
and a temple of the Holy Spirit.

Help him (her) in all the dangers of this life
and strengthen him (her) in the constant effort to
reach your kingdom,
through the power of Christ our Savior.
We ask this through Christ our Lord.

All:
Amen.

EXPLANATORY RITES

ANOINTING AFTER BAPTISM

178. Then the celebrant says:

God the Father of our Lord Jesus Christ has freed you
from sin, given you a new birth by water and the Holy
Spirit, and welcomed you into his holy people. He now
anoints you with the chrism of salvation. As Christ was
anointed Priest, Prophet, and King, so may you live
always as a member of his body, sharing everlasting life.

All:
Amen.

Then the celebrant anoints the child on the crown of the head with the chrism, in silence.

CLOTHING WITH WHITE GARMENT

179. The celebrant says:

N., you have become a new creation, and have clothed yourself in Christ.

See in this white garment the outward sign of your Christian dignity. With your family and friends to help you by word and example, bring that dignity unstained into the everlasting life of heaven.

All:

Amen.

LIGHTED CANDLE

180. The celebrant takes the Easter candle and says:

Receive the light of Christ.

Someone, such as the father or godfather, lights the child's candle from the Easter candle.

The celebrant then says:

Parents and godparents, this light is entrusted to you to be kept burning brightly. This child of yours has been enlightened by Christ. He (she) is to walk always as a child of the light. May he (she) keep the flame of faith alive in his (her) heart. When the Lord comes, may he (she) go out to meet him with all the saints in the heavenly kingdom.

A baptismal song is appropriate at this time, such as:

You have put on Christ,
in him you have been baptized.
Alleluia, alleluia.

Other songs may be chosen from nos. 225–245, pages 159–161.

CONCLUSION OF THE RITE

LORD'S PRAYER

181. The celebrant stands in front of the altar and addresses the parents, godparents, and the whole assembly in these or similar words:

My dear brothers and sisters, this child has been reborn in baptism. He (she) is now called the child of God, for so indeed he (she) is. In confirmation he (she) will receive the fullness of God's Spirit. In holy communion he (she) will share the banquet of Christ's sacrifice, calling God his (her) Father in the midst of the Church. In the name of this child, in the spirit of our common sonship, let us pray together in the words our Lord has given us:

182. All present join the celebrant in singing or saying:

**Our Father,
who art in heaven,
hallowed be thy name;
thy kingdom come;
thy will be done on earth as it is in heaven.
Give us this day our daily bread;
and forgive us our trespasses
as we forgive those who trespass against us;
and lead us not into temptation,
but deliver us from evil.**

BLESSING AND DISMISSAL

183. The celebrant first blesses the mother, who holds the child in her arms, then the father, and lastly the entire assembly:

Celebrant:

God the Father, through his Son, the Virgin Mary's child, has brought joy to all Christian mothers, as they see the hope of eternal life shine on their children.

May he bless the mother of this child. She now thanks God for the gift of her child. May she be one with her son (daughter) in thanking God for ever in heaven, in Christ Jesus our Lord.

All:

Amen.

Celebrant:

God is the giver of all life, human and divine. May he bless the father of this child. He and his wife will be the first teachers of their child in the ways of faith. May they also be the best of teachers, bearing witness to the faith by what they say and do, in Christ Jesus our Lord.

All:

Amen.

Celebrant:

By God's gift, through water and the Holy Spirit, we are reborn to everlasting life. In his goodness, may he continue to pour out his blessings on these sons and daughters of his. May he make them always, wherever they may be, faithful members of his holy people. May he send his peace upon all who are gathered here, in Christ Jesus our Lord.

All:

Amen.

Celebrant:

May almighty God, the Father, and the Son, ✝ and the Holy Spirit, bless you.

All:

Amen.

Celebrant:

Go in peace.

All:

Thanks be to God.

For other forms of the blessing, see nos. 247–249, pages **162–164**.

184. After the blessing, all may sing a hymn which suitably expresses thanksgiving and Easter joy, or they may sing the song of the Blessed Virgin Mary, the Magnificat.

Where there is the practice of bringing the baptized child to the altar of the blessed Virgin, this custom is observed if appropriate.

185. The above rite is followed even when the baptized child is brought to the church after other difficulties (such as persecution, disagreement between parents) which prevented the celebration of baptism in the church. In such cases, the celebrant should adapt the explanations, readings, intentions in the prayer of the faithful and other parts of the rite to the child's circumstances.

VARIOUS TEXTS FOR USE IN THE CELEBRATION OF BAPTISM FOR CHILDREN

CHAPTER VII
VARIOUS TEXTS FOR USE IN THE CELEBRATION OF BAPTISM FOR CHILDREN

I. SCRIPTURAL READINGS

OLD TESTAMENT READINGS

186   Exodus 17:3-7

A reading from the Book of Exodus

Give us water to drink (Exodus 17:2).

In their thirst for water,
    the people grumbled against Moses,
    saying, "Why did you ever make us leave Egypt?
Was it just to have us die here of thirst
    with our children and our livestock?"
So Moses cried out to the LORD,
    "What shall I do with this people?
A little more and they will stone me!"
The LORD answered Moses,
    "Go over there in front of the people,
    along with some of the elders of Israel,
    holding in your hand, as you go,
    the staff with which you struck the river.
I will be standing there in front of you on the rock
    in Horeb.
Strike the rock, and the water will flow from it
    for the people to drink."
This Moses did, in the presence of the elders of Israel.
The place was called Massah and Meribah,
    because the children of Israel quarreled there
    and tested the LORD, saying,
    "Is the LORD in our midst or not?"

The word of the Lord.

187   Ezekiel 36:24-28

A reading from the Book of the Prophet Ezekiel

I shall pour clean water upon you to cleanse you from all your impurities.

Thus says the Lord GOD:

I will take you away from among the nations,
> **gather you from all the foreign lands,**
> **and bring you back to your own land.**

I will sprinkle clean water upon you
> **to cleanse you from all your impurities,**
> **and from all your idols I will cleanse you.**

I will give you a new heart and place a new spirit
> > **within you,**
> **taking from your bodies your stony hearts**
> **and giving you natural hearts.**

I will put my spirit within you and make you live by
> > **my statutes,**
> **careful to observe my decrees.**

You shall live in the land I gave your fathers;
> **you shall be my people, and I will be your God.**

The word of the Lord.

188   Ezekiel 47:1-9, 12

A reading from the Book of the Prophet Ezekiel

I saw water flowing from the temple, and all who were touched by it were saved (see *Roman Missal,* antiphon for blessing and sprinkling holy water during the season of Easter).

The angel brought me, Ezekiel,
> **back to the entrance of the temple of the Lord,**
> **and I saw water flowing out**
> **from beneath the threshold of the temple toward**
> > **the east,**
> **for the façade of the temple was toward the east;**
> **the water flowed down from the right side of the**
> > **temple,**

south of the altar.
He led me outside by the north gate,
and around to the outer gate facing the east,
where I saw water trickling from the right side.
Then when he had walked off to the east
with a measuring cord in his hand,
he measured off a thousand cubits
and had me wade through the water,
which was ankle-deep.
He measured off another thousand
and once more had me wade through the water,
which was now knee-deep.
Again he measured off a thousand and had me wade;
the water was up to my waist.
Once more he measured off a thousand,
but there was now a river through which I could
not wade;
for the water had risen so high it had become a river
that could not be crossed except by swimming.
He asked me, "Have you seen this, son of man?"
Then he brought me to the bank of the river, where he
had me sit.
Along the bank of the river I saw very many trees on
both sides.
He said to me,
"This water flows into the eastern district down
upon the Arabah,
and empties into the sea, the salt waters, which it
makes fresh.
Wherever the river flows,
every sort of living creature that can multiply
shall live,
and there shall be abundant fish,

for wherever this water comes the sea shall be
made fresh.
Along both banks of the river, fruit trees of every kind
shall grow;
their leaves shall not fade, nor their fruit fail.
Every month they shall bear fresh fruit,
for they shall be watered by the flow from the
sanctuary.
Their fruit shall serve for food, and their leaves for
medicine."

The word of the Lord.

NEW TESTAMENT READINGS

189   Romans 6:3-5

A reading from the Letter of Saint Paul to the Romans

Buried with him through baptism into death, we too might live in newness of life.

Brothers and sisters:
Are you unaware that we who were baptized into
Christ Jesus
were baptized into his death?
We were indeed buried with him through baptism
into death,
so that, just as Christ was raised from the dead
by the glory of the Father,
we too might live in newness of life.

For if we have grown into union with him through a
death like his,
we shall also be united with him in the resurrection.

The word of the Lord.

190   Romans 8:28-32

A reading from the Letter of Saint Paul to the Romans

To be conformed to the image of his Son.

Brothers and sisters:

We know that all things work for good for those who
         love God,
      who are called according to his purpose.

For those he foreknew he also predestined
      to be conformed to the image of his Son,
      so that he might be the firstborn
      among many brothers.

And those he predestined he also called;
      and those he called he also justified;
      and those he justified he also glorified.

What then shall we say to this?
If God is for us, who can be against us?
He who did not spare his own Son
      but handed him over for us all,
      how will he not also give us everything else along
         with him?

The word of the Lord.

191   1 Corinthians 12:12-13

**A reading from the first Letter of Saint Paul to the
Corinthians**

For in one Spirit we were all baptized into one Body.

Brothers and sisters:

As a body is one though it has many parts,
      and all the parts of the body, though many, are
            one body,
      so also Christ.

For in one Spirit we were all baptized into one Body,
      whether Jews or Greeks, slaves or free persons,
      and we were all given to drink of one Spirit.

The word of the Lord.

192   Galatians 3:26-28

A reading from the Letter of Saint Paul to the Galatians

All of you who were baptized into Christ have clothed yourselves with Christ.

Brothers and sisters:
Through faith you are all children of God in Christ Jesus.
For all of you who were baptized into Christ
    have clothed yourselves with Christ.
There is neither Jew nor Greek,
        there is neither slave nor free person,
        there is not male and female;
        for you are all one in Christ Jesus.

The word of the Lord.

193   Ephesians 4:1-6

A reading from the Letter of Saint Paul to the Ephesians

There is one Lord, one faith, one baptism.

Brothers and sisters:
I, a prisoner for the Lord,
        urge you to live in a manner worthy of the call you
            have received,
        with all humility and gentleness, with patience,
        bearing with one another through love,
        striving to preserve the unity of the spirit
        through the bond of peace:
        one Body and one Spirit,
        as you were also called to the one hope of your call;
        one Lord, one faith, one baptism;
        one God and Father of all,
        who is over all and through all and in all.

The word of the Lord.

A reading from the first Letter of Saint Peter

You are a chosen race, a royal priesthood.

Beloved:

Come to the Lord, a living stone, rejected by human
     beings
    but chosen and precious in the sight of God,
    and, like living stones,
    let yourselves be built into a spiritual house
    to be a holy priesthood to offer spiritual sacrifices
     acceptable to God through Jesus Christ.

You are *a chosen race, a royal priesthood,*
    a holy nation, a people of his own,
    ***so that you may announce the praises* of him**
    who called you out of darkness into his wonderful
     light.

Once you were *no people*
    but now you are God's people;
you *had not received mercy*
    but now you have received mercy.

The word of the Lord.

RESPONSORIAL PSALMS

195 Psalm 23:1-3a, 3b-4, 5, 6

℞. (1) **The Lord is my shepherd;**
there is nothing I shall want.

The LORD is my shepherd; I shall not want.
In verdant pastures he gives me repose;
Beside restful waters he leads me;
he refreshes my soul.
℞. The Lord is my shepherd; there is nothing I shall want.

He guides me in right paths
for his name's sake.
Even though I walk in the dark valley
I fear no evil; for you are at my side
With your rod and your staff
that give me courage.
℞. The Lord is my shepherd; there is nothing I shall want.

You spread the table before me
in the sight of my foes;
You anoint my head with oil;
my cup overflows.
℞. The Lord is my shepherd; there is nothing I shall want.

Only goodness and kindness follow me
all the days of my life;
And I shall dwell in the house of the LORD
for years to come.
℞. The Lord is my shepherd; there is nothing I shall want.

Psalm 27:1bcde, 4, 8b-9abc, 13-14

℞. (1b) **The Lord is my light and my salvation.**

or: (Ephesians 5:14) **Wake up and rise from death:**
Christ will shine upon you!

The Lord is my light and my salvation;
whom should I fear?
The Lord is my life's refuge;
of whom should I be afraid?

℞. The Lord is my light and my salvation.

or: Wake up and rise from death: Christ will shine upon you!

One thing I ask of the Lord;
this I seek:
To dwell in the house of the Lord
all the days of my life,
That I may gaze on the loveliness of the Lord
and contemplate his temple.

℞. The Lord is my light and my salvation.

or: Wake up and rise from death: Christ will shine upon you!

Your presence, O Lord, I seek.
Hide not your face from me;
do not in anger repel your servant.
You are my helper: cast me not off.

℞. The Lord is my light and my salvation.

or: Wake up and rise from death: Christ will shine upon you!

I believe that I shall see the bounty of the Lord
in the land of the living.
Wait for the Lord with courage;
be stouthearted, and wait for the Lord.

℞. The Lord is my light and my salvation.

or: Wake up and rise from death: Christ will shine upon you!

197 Psalm 34:2-3, 6-7, 8-9, 14-15, 16-17, 18-19

℟. (6a) **Look to him, that you may be radiant with joy!**
or: (9a) **Taste and see the goodness of the Lord.**

I will bless the Lord at all times;
his praise shall be ever in my mouth.
Let my soul glory in the Lord;
the lowly will hear me and be glad.
℟. Look to him, that you may be radiant with joy!
or: Taste and see the goodness of the Lord.

Look to him that you may be radiant with joy,
and your faces may not blush with shame.
When the poor one called out, the Lord heard,
and from all his distress he saved him.
℟. Look to him, that you may be radiant with joy!
or: Taste and see the goodness of the Lord.

The angel of the Lord encamps
around those who fear him, and delivers them.
Taste and see how good the Lord is;
happy the man who takes refuge in him.
℟. Look to him, that you may be radiant with joy!
or: Taste and see the goodness of the Lord.

Keep your tongue from evil
and your lips from speaking guile;
Turn from evil, and do good;
seek peace, and follow after it.
℟. Look to him, that you may be radiant with joy!
or: Taste and see the goodness of the Lord.

The Lord has eyes for the just
and ears for their cry.
The Lord confronts the evildoers,
to destroy remembrance of them from the earth.
℟. Look to him, that you may be radiant with joy!
or: Taste and see the goodness of the Lord.

When the just cry out, the Lord hears them,
> **and from all their distress he rescues them.**
The Lord is close to the brokenhearted,
> **and those who are crushed in spirit he saves.**
℟. Look to him, that you may be radiant with joy!
or: Taste and see the goodness of the Lord.

Alleluia Verse and Verse Before the Gospel

Outside of Lent, the cantor sings **Alleluia**; it is then repeated by the people. The cantor then sings one of the verses given below, nos. 198–203, and the people repeat **Alleluia**.

During Lent, the same pattern is followed, except that one of the following invocations replaces the **Alleluia**:

(a) Praise to you, Lord Jesus Christ, king of endless glory!
(b) Praise and honor to you, Lord Jesus Christ!
(c) Glory and praise to you, Lord Jesus Christ!
(d) Glory to you, Word of God, Lord Jesus Christ!

198   John 3:16

God so loved the world that he gave his only-begotton
> **Son,**
so that everyone who believes in him might have
> **eternal life.**

199   John 8:12

I am the light of the world, says the Lord;
whoever follows me will have the light of life.

200   John 14:6

I am the way and the truth and the life, says the Lord;
no one comes to the Father, except through me.

201   Ephesians 4:5-6a

There is one Lord, one faith, one baptism,
one God and the Father of all.

202   See 2 Timothy 1:10

Our Savior Jesus Christ has destroyed death
and brought life to light through the Gospel.

203   1 Peter 2:9

You are a chosen race, a royal priesthood, a holy nation:
announce the praises of him who called you
out of darkness into his wonderful light.

GOSPEL

204   Matthew 22:35-40

A reading from the holy Gospel according to Matthew

This is the greatest and the first commandment.

One of the Pharisees, a scholar of the law, tested Jesus
        by asking,
    "Teacher, which commandment in the law is the
            greatest?"
He said to him,
    "You shall love the Lord, your God, with all your
            heart,
    with all your soul, and with all your mind.
This is the greatest and the first commandment.
The second is like it:
    You shall love your neighbor as yourself.
The whole law and the prophets depend on these two
        commandments."

The Gospel of the Lord.

205   Matthew 28:18-20

A reading from the holy Gospel according to Matthew

Go, therefore, and make disciples of all nations, baptizing them in the
name of the Father, and of the Son, and of the Holy Spirit.

Jesus said to the Eleven disciples:
"All power in heaven and on earth has been given to me.
Go, therefore, and make disciples of all nations,
    baptizing them in the name of the Father,
    and of the Son, and of the Holy Spirit,
    teaching them to observe all that I have commanded
        you.

**And behold, I am with you always, until the end of
the age."**

The Gospel of the Lord.

206   Mark 1:9-11

A reading from the holy Gospel according to Mark

Jesus was baptized in the Jordan by John.

**Jesus came from Nazareth of Galilee
and was baptized in the Jordan by John.
On coming up out of the water he saw the heavens
being torn open
and the Spirit, like a dove, descending upon him.
And a voice came from the heavens,
"You are my beloved Son; with you I am well
pleased."**

The Gospel of the Lord.

207   Mark 10:13-16

A reading from the holy Gospel according to Mark

Let the children come to me; do not prevent them.

**People were bringing children to Jesus that he might
touch them,
but the disciples rebuked them.
When Jesus saw this he became indignant and said to
them,
"Let the children come to me; do not prevent them,
for the Kingdom of God belongs to such as these.
Amen, I say to you,
whoever does not accept the Kingdom of God like
a child
will not enter it."
Then he embraced them and blessed them,
placing his hands on them.**

The Gospel of the Lord.

208 Mark 12:28-34 *or* 12:28-31

A reading from the holy Gospel according to Mark

Hear O Israel! You shall love the Lord, your God, with all your heart.

LONG FORM

One of the scribes came to Jesus and asked him,
"Which is the first of all the commandments?"
Jesus replied, "The first is this:
Hear, O Israel!
The Lord our God is Lord alone!
You shall love the Lord your God with all your heart,
with all your soul, with all your mind,
and with all your strength.
The second is this:
You shall love your neighbor as yourself.
There is no other commandment greater than these."
The scribe said to him,
"Well said, teacher. You are right in saying,
'He is One and there is no other than he.'
And 'to love him with all your heart,
with all your understanding,
with all your strength,
and to love your neighbor as yourself'
is worth more than all burnt offerings and sacrifices."
And when Jesus saw that he answered with
understanding,
he said to him,
"You are not far from the Kingdom of God."
And no one dared to ask him any more questions.

The Gospel of the Lord.

or:

SHORT FORM

One of the scribes came to Jesus and asked him,
"Which is the first of all the commandments?"

Jesus replied, "The first is this:

'Hear, O Israel! The Lord our God is Lord alone!
You shall love the Lord your God with all your heart,
with all your soul, with all your mind,
and with all your strength.'

The second is this:

'You shall love your neighbor as yourself.'

There is no other commandment greater than these."

The Gospel of the Lord.

209   John 3:1-6

A reading from the holy Gospel according to John

No one can see the Kingdom of God without being born from above.

There was a Pharisee named Nicodemus, a ruler of
    the Jews.
He came to Jesus at night and said to him,
    "Rabbi, we know that you are a teacher who has
        come from God,
    for no one can do these signs that you are doing
    unless God is with him."
Jesus answered and said to him,
    "Amen, amen, I say to you,
    unless one is born from above,
    he cannot see the Kingdom of God."
Nicodemus said to him,
    "How can a man once grown old be born again?
Surely he cannot reenter his mother's womb and be
    born again, can he?"
Jesus answered,
    "Amen, amen, I say to you,
    unless one is born of water and Spirit
    he cannot enter the Kingdom of God.
What is born of flesh is flesh
    and what is born of spirit is spirit."
The Gospel of the Lord.

210 John 4:5-14

A reading from the holy Gospel according to John

A spring of water welling up to eternal life.

Jesus came to a town of Samaria called Sychar,
near the plot of land that Jacob had given to his
son Joseph.
Jacob's well was there.
Jesus, tired from his journey, sat down there at
the well.
It was about noon.

A woman of Samaria came to draw water.
Jesus said to her,
"Give me a drink."
His disciples had gone into the town to buy food.
The Samaritan woman said to him,
"How can you, a Jew, ask me, a Samaritan woman,
for a drink?"
—For Jews use nothing in common with Samaritans.—
Jesus answered and said to her,
"If you knew the gift of God
and who is saying to you, 'Give me a drink,'
you would have asked him
and he would have given you living water."
The woman said to him,
"Sir, you do not even have a bucket and the cistern
is deep;
where then can you get this living water?
Are you greater than our father Jacob,
who gave us this cistern and drank from it himself
with his children and his flocks?"
Jesus answered and said to her,
"Everyone who drinks this water will be thirsty again;
but whoever drinks the water I shall give will never
thirst;

the water I shall give will become in him
a spring of water welling up to eternal life."
The Gospel of the Lord.

211   John 6:44-47

A reading from the holy Gospel according to John

Whoever believes has eternal life.

Jesus said to the crowds:
"No one can come to me unless the Father who sent
**   me draw him,**
**   and I shall raise him on the last day.**
It is written in the prophets:

> ***They shall all be taught by God.***

Everyone who listens to my Father and learns from
**   him comes to me.**
Not that anyone has seen the Father
**   except the one who is from God;**
**   he has seen the Father.**
Amen, amen, I say to you,
**   whoever believes has eternal life."**
The Gospel of the Lord.

212   John 7:37b-39a

A reading from the holy Gospel according to John

Rivers of living water will flow.

Jesus stood up and exclaimed,
**   "Let anyone who thirsts come to me and drink.**
Whoever believes in me, as Scripture says:

> ***Rivers of living water will flow from within him."***

He said this in reference to the Spirit
**   that those who came to believe in him were**
**   to receive.**
The Gospel of the Lord.

213   John 9:1-7

A reading from the holy Gospel according to John

So he went and washed and came back able to see.

As Jesus passed by he saw a man blind from birth.
His disciples asked him,
  "Rabbi, who sinned, this man or his parents,
  that he was born blind?"
Jesus answered,
  "Neither he nor his parents sinned;
  it is so that the works of God might be made visible
    through him.
We have to do the works of the one who sent me while
    it is day.
Night is coming when no one can work.
While I am in the world, I am the light of the world."
When he had said this, he spat on the ground
  and made clay with the saliva,
  and smeared the clay on his eyes, and said to him,
  "Go wash in the Pool of Siloam" (which means Sent).
So he went and washed, and came back able to see.

The Gospel of the Lord.

214   John 15:1-11

A reading from the holy Gospel according to John

Whoever remains in me and I in him will bear much fruit.

Jesus said to his disciples:
"I am the true vine, and my Father is the vine grower.
He takes away every branch in me that does not
    bear fruit,
  and everyone that does he prunes so that it bears
    more fruit.
You are already pruned because of the word that I
    spoke to you.

Remain in me, as I remain in you.
Just as a branch cannot bear fruit on its own
    unless it remains on the vine,
    so neither can you unless you remain in me.
I am the vine, you are the branches.
Whoever remains in me and I in him will bear
    much fruit,
    because without me you can do nothing.
Anyone who does not remain in me
    will be thrown out like a branch and wither;
    people will gather them and throw them into a fire
    and they will be burned.
If you remain in me and my words remain in you,
    ask for whatever you want and it will be done for you.
By this is my Father glorified,
    that you bear much fruit and become my disciples.
As the Father loves me, so I also love you.
Remain in my love.
If you keep my commandments, you will remain in
    my love,
    just as I have kept my Father's commandments
    and remain in his love.

"I have told you this so that my joy may be in you
    and your joy may be complete."

The Gospel of the Lord.

215 John 19:31-35

A reading from the holy Gospel according to John

One soldier thrust his lance into his side, and immediately Blood and water flowed out.

Since it was preparation day,
> **in order that the bodies might not remain on the**
>> **cross on the sabbath,**
> **for the sabbath day of that week was a solemn one,**
> **the Jews asked Pilate that their legs be broken**
> **and they be taken down.**

So the soldiers came and broke the legs of the first
> **and then of the other one who was crucified with**
>> **Jesus.**

But when they came to Jesus and saw that he was
> **already dead,**
> **they did not break his legs,**
> **but one soldier thrust his lance into his side,**
> **and immediately Blood and water flowed out.**

An eyewitness has testified, and his testimony is true;
> **he knows that he is speaking the truth,**
> **so that you also may come to believe.**

The Gospel of the Lord.

II. OTHER FORMS OF THE GENERAL INTERCESSIONS

Any one of the following forms given in this baptismal ritual may be used for the general intercessions. Petitions may be added or omitted at will, taking into consideration the special circumstances of each family. The prayer always concludes with the invocation of the saints.

1   216. As given above in no. 47, page 27.

2 217

We have been called by the Lord to be a royal priesthood, a holy nation, a people he has acquired for himself. Let us ask him to show his mercy to these children, who are to receive the graces of baptism, to their parents and godparents, and to all the baptized everywhere.

Through baptism, bring these children into your Church.
℞. Lord, hear our prayer.

Throughout their lives, help them to be faithful witnesses to your Son, Jesus Christ, for they are being marked with his cross.
℞. Lord, hear our prayer.

As they are being buried in the likeness of Christ's death through baptism, may they also share in the glory of Christ's resurrection.
℞. Lord, hear our prayer.

Teach them by the words and example of their parents and godparents, and help them to grow strong as living members of the Church.
℞. Lord, hear our prayer.

Renew the grace of baptism in each of us here.
℞. Lord, hear our prayer.

May all Christ's followers, baptized into one body, always live united in faith and love.
℞. Lord, hear our prayer.

The invocation of the saints follows, page 167.

3 218

My fellow Christians, let us ask the mercy of Jesus Christ our Lord for these children who will receive the gift of baptism, for their parents and godparents, and for all baptized persons.

Through baptism, make these children God's own sons and daughters.
℟. Lord, hear our prayer.

Help these tender branches grow to be more like you, the true vine, and be your faithful followers.
℟. Lord, hear our prayer.

May they always keep your commands, walk in your love, and proclaim your Good News to their fellow men.
℟. Lord, hear our prayer.

May they be counted as God's friends through your saving work, Lord Jesus, and may they inherit eternal life.
℟. Lord, hear our prayer.

Help their parents and godparents to lead them to know and love God.
℟. Lord, hear our prayer.

Inspire all men to share in the new birth of baptism.
℟. Lord, hear our prayer.

The invocation of the saints follows, page 167.

4   219

We have been called by the Lord to be a royal priesthood, a holy nation, a people he has acquired for himself. Let us ask him to show his mercy to these children, who are to receive the graces of baptism, to their parents and godparents, and to all the baptized everywhere.

Through baptism may these children become God's own beloved sons and daughters. We pray to the Lord.
R̸. Lord, hear our prayer.

Once they are born again of water and the Holy Spirit, may they always live in that Spirit, and make their new life known to their fellow men. We pray to the Lord.
R̸. Lord, hear our prayer.

Help them to triumph over the deceits of the devil and the attractions of evil. We pray to the Lord.
R̸. Lord, hear our prayer.

May they love you, Lord, with all their heart, soul, mind and strength, and love their neighbor as themselves. We pray to the Lord.
R̸. Lord, hear our prayer.

Help all of us here to be models of faith for these children. We pray to the Lord.
R̸. Lord, hear our prayer.

May all Christ's faithful people, who received the sign of the cross at baptism, always and everywhere give witness to him by the way they live. We pray to the Lord.
R̸. Lord, hear our prayer.

The invocation of the saints follows, page 167.

5 220

Let us ask Christ's mercy for these children, their parents and godparents, and all baptized Christians.

Give them a new birth to eternal life through water and the Holy Spirit.
℞. Lord, hear our prayer.

Help them always to be living members of your Church.
℞. Lord, hear our prayer.

Inspire them to hear and follow your gospel, and to give witness to you by their lives. We ask this, Lord.
℞. Lord, hear our prayer.

May they come with joy to the table of your sacrifice.
℞. Lord, hear our prayer.

Help them to love God and neighbor as you have taught us.
℞. Lord, hear our prayer.

May they grow in holiness and wisdom by listening to their fellow Christians and by following their example.
℞. Lord, hear our prayer.

Let all your followers remain united in faith and love.
℞. Lord, hear our prayer.

The invocation of the saints follows, page 167.

III. ANOTHER FORM OF THE PRAYER OF EXORCISM

221   **Almighty God,**
you sent your only Son
to rescue us from the slavery of sin,
and to give us the freedom
only your sons and daughters enjoy.

We now pray for these children
who will have to face the world with its temptations,
and fight the devil in all his cunning.

Your Son died and rose again to save us.
By his victory over sin and death,
cleanse these children from the stain of original sin.
Strengthen them with the grace of Christ,
and watch over them at every step in life's journey.
We ask this through Christ our Lord.

     All:
Amen.

IV. BLESSING AND INVOCATION OF GOD OVER BAPTISMAL WATER

1   222. See the formula in no. 54a, page 84.

2   223

Celebrant:

Praise to you, almighty God and Father, for you have created water to cleanse and to give life.

All:

Blessed be God (or some other suitable acclamation by the people).

Celebrant:

Praise to you, Lord Jesus Christ, the Father's only Son, for you offered yourself on the cross, that in the blood and water flowing from your side, and through your death and resurrection, the Church might be born.

All:

Blessed be God.

Celebrant:

Praise to you, God the Holy Spirit, for you anointed Christ at his baptism in the waters of Jordan, so that we might all be baptized into you.

All:

Blessed be God.

Celebrant:

* Come to us, Lord, Father of all, and make holy this water which you have created, so that all who are baptized in it may be washed clean of sin, and be born again to live as your children.

All:

Hear us, Lord (or some other suitable invocation).

Celebrant:

Make this water holy, Lord, so that all who are baptized into Christ's death and resurrection by this water may become more perfectly like your Son.

All:

Hear us, Lord.

The celebrant touches the water with his right hand and continues:

Lord, make holy this water which you have created, so that all those whom you have chosen may be born again by the power of the Holy Spirit, and may take their place among your holy people.

All:

Hear us, Lord.

* If the baptismal water has already been blessed the celebrant omits the invocation Come to us, Lord and those which follow it and says:

You have called your children, N., N., to this cleansing water that they may share in the faith of your Church and have eternal life. By the mystery of this consecrated water lead them to a new and spiritual birth. (We ask this) through Christ our Lord.

All:

Amen.

3   224

Celebrant:

Father, God of mercy, through these waters of baptism you have filled us with new life as your very own children.

All:

Blessed be God (or some other suitable acclamation by the people).

Celebrant:

From all who are baptized in water and the Holy Spirit, you have formed one people, united in your Son Jesus Christ.

All:

Blessed be God.

Celebrant:

You have set us free and filled our hearts with the Spirit of your love, that we may live in your peace.

All:

Blessed be God.

Celebrant:

You call those who have been baptized to announce the Good News of Jesus Christ to people everywhere.

All:

Blessed be God.

Unblessed Celebrant:

* You have called your children, N., N., to this cleansing water and new birth that by sharing the faith of your Church (they) might have eternal life. Bless ✢ this water in which (they) will be baptized. We ask this in the name of Christ our Lord.

All:

Amen.   Pg. 61

> * If the baptismal water has already been blessed, the celebrant omits this last prayer and says:
>
> **You have called your children, N., N., to this cleansing water that (they) may share in the faith of your Church and have eternal life. By the mystery of this consecrated water lead (them) to a new and spiritual birth. (We ask this) through Christ our Lord.**
>
> All:
> Amen.

[handwritten: Blessed]

[handwritten: N.]

[handwritten: Pg. 61]

V. ACCLAMATIONS AND HYMNS

ACCLAMATIONS FROM SACRED SCRIPTURE

225   **Lord God, who is your equal?**   Exodus 15:11
      Strong, majestic, and holy!
      Worthy of praise, worker of wonders!

226   **God is light: in him there is no darkness.**   1 John 1:5

227   **God is love: he who lives in love,**   1 John 4:16
        lives in God.

228   **There is one God, one Father of all:**   Ephesians 4:6
      he is over all, and through all:
      he lives in all of us.

229   **Come to him and receive his light!**   Psalm 34:6

230   **Blessed be God**   see Ephesians 1:4
        who chose you in Christ.

231   **You are God's work of art,**   Ephesians 2:10
        created in Christ Jesus.

232 **You are now God's children,**
 my dearest friends.
What you shall be in his glory
 has not yet been revealed.

1 John 3:2

233 **Think of how God loves you!**
He calls you his own children,
and that is what you are.

1 John 3:1

234 **Happy are those who have**
 washed their robes clean:
washed in the blood of the Lamb!

Revelation 22:14

235 **All of you are one:**
united in Christ Jesus.

Galatians 3:28

236 **Imitate God, walk in his love,**
just as Christ loves us.

Ephesians 5:1-2

HYMNS IN THE STYLE OF THE NEW TESTAMENT

237 **Praised be the Father**
 of our Lord Jesus Christ:
a God so merciful and kind!
He has given us a new birth, a living hope,
by raising Jesus his Son from death.
Salvation is our undying inheritance,
preserved for us in heaven,
salvation at the end of time.

1 Peter 1:3-5

238 **How great the sign of God's love for us,**
Jesus Christ our Lord:
promised before all time began,
revealed in these last days.
He lived and suffered and died for us,
but the Spirit raised him to life.

> **People everywhere have heard his message**
> **and placed their faith in him.**
> **What wonderful blessings he gives his people:**
> **living in the Father's glory,**
> **he fills all creation**
> **and guides it to perfection.**

Songs from Ancient Liturgies

239 **We believe in you, Lord Jesus Christ.**
Fill our hearts with your radiance,
and make us the children of light!

240 **We come to you, Lord Jesus.**
Fill us with your life,
make us children of the Father,
and one in you.

241 **Lord Jesus, from your wounded side**
flowed streams of cleansing water:
the world was washed of all its sin,
all life made new again!

242 **The Father's voice calls us above the waters,**
the glory of the Son shines on us,
the love of the Spirit fills us with life.

243 **Holy Church of God, stretch out your hand**
and welcome your children
newborn of water
and of the Spirit of God.

244 **Rejoice, you newly baptized,**
chosen members of the kingdom.
Buried with Christ in death,
you are reborn in him by faith.

245 **This is the fountain of life,**
water made holy by the suffering of Christ,
washing all the world.
You who are washed in this water
have hope of heaven's kingdom.

VI. FORMS OF THE FINAL BLESSING

1 246. See the formula in the rite of baptism for several children, no. 70, page 45.

2 247

Celebrant:

May God the almighty Father, who filled the world with joy by giving us his only Son, bless these newly-baptized children. May they grow to be more fully like Jesus Christ our Lord.

All:

Amen.

Celebrant:

May almighty God, who gives life on earth and in heaven, bless the parents of these children. They thank him now for the gift he has given them. May they always show that gratitude in action by loving and caring for their children.

All:

Amen.

Celebrant:

May almighty God, who has given us a new birth by water and the Holy Spirit, generously bless all of us who are his faithful children. May we always live as his people, and may he bless all here present with his peace.

All:

Amen.

Celebrant:

May almighty God, the Father, and the Son, ✠ and the Holy Spirit, bless you.

All:

Amen.

3   248

Celebrant:

May God, the source of life and love, who fills the hearts of mothers with love for their children, bless the mothers of these newly-baptized children. As they thank God for a safe delivery, may they find joy in the love, growth, and holiness of their children.

All:

Amen.

Celebrant:

May God, the Father and model of all fathers, help these fathers to give good example, so that their children will grow to be mature Christians in all the fullness of Jesus Christ.

All:

Amen.

Celebrant:

May God, who loves all people, bless all the relatives and friends who are gathered here. In his mercy, may he guard them from evil and give them his abundant peace.

All:

Amen.

Celebrant:

And may almighty God, the Father, and the Son, ✠ and the Holy Spirit, bless you.

All:

Amen.

4   249

Celebrant:

My brothers and sisters, we entrust you all to the mercy and help of God the almighty Father, his only Son, and the Holy Spirit. May he watch over your life, and may we all walk by the light of faith, and attain the good things he has promised us.

Go in peace, and may almighty God, the Father, and the Son, ✠ and the Holy Spirit, bless you.

All:

Amen.

LITANY OF THE SAINTS

LITANY OF THE SAINTS

LITANY FOR SOLEMN INTERCESSIONS

In those sections which contain several sets of invocations marked by A and B, one or the other may be chosen as desired. The names of other saints may be added in the appropriate place in the litany (for example, patrons, titles of churches, founders, etc.), but in a different kind of type. Some petitions adapted to the place and need may be added to the petitions for various needs.

I. PRAYER TO GOD

A **Lord, have mercy.**   **Lord, have mercy.**
   Christ, have mercy.   **Christ, have mercy.**
   Lord, have mercy.   **Lord, have mercy.**

B **God our Father in heaven,**   **have mercy on us.**
   God the Son, our redeemer,   **have mercy on us.**
   God the Holy Spirit,   **have mercy on us.**
   Holy Trinity, one God,   **have mercy on us.**

II. INVOCATION OF THE SAINTS

Holy Mary,   **pray for us.**
Mother of God,   **pray for us.**
Most honored of all virgins,   **pray for us.**
Michael, Gabriel, and Raphael,   **pray for us.**
Angels of God,   **pray for us.**

PROPHETS AND FATHERS OF OUR FAITH

Abraham, Moses, and Elijah,   **pray for us.**
Saint John the Baptist,   **pray for us.**
Saint Joseph,   **pray for us.**
Holy patriarchs and prophets,   **pray for us.**

Apostles and Followers of Christ

Saint Peter and Saint Paul,	**pray for us.**
Saint Andrew,	**pray for us.**
Saint John and Saint James,	**pray for us.**
Saint Thomas,	**pray for us.**
Saint Matthew,	**pray for us.**
All holy apostles,	**pray for us.**
Saint Luke,	**pray for us.**
Saint Mark,	**pray for us.**
Saint Barnabas,	**pray for us.**
Saint Mary Magdalene,	**pray for us.**
All disciples of the Lord,	**pray for us.**

Martyrs

Saint Stephen,	**pray for us.**
Saint Ignatius,	**pray for us.**
Saint Polycarp,	**pray for us.**
Saint Justin,	**pray for us.**
Saint Lawrence,	**pray for us.**
Saint Cyprian,	**pray for us.**
Saint Boniface,	**pray for us.**
Saint Stanislaus,	**pray for us.**
Saint Thomas Becket,	**pray for us.**
Saint John Fisher and Saint Thomas More,	**pray for us.**
Saint Paul Miki,	**pray for us.**
Saint Isaac Jogues and	
Saint John de Brebeuf,	**pray for us.**
Saint Peter Chanel,	**pray for us.**
Saint Charles Lwanga,	**pray for us.**
Saint Perpetua and Saint Felicity,	**pray for us.**
Saint Agnes,	**pray for us.**
Saint Maria Goretti,	**pray for us.**
All holy martyrs for Christ,	**pray for us.**

BISHOPS AND DOCTORS

Saint Leo and Saint Gregory,   pray for us.
Saint Ambrose,   pray for us.
Saint Jerome,   pray for us.
Saint Augustine,   pray for us.
Saint Athanasius,   pray for us.
Saint Basil and Saint Gregory,   pray for us.
Saint John Chrysostom,   pray for us.
Saint Martin,   pray for us.
Saint Patrick,   pray for us.
Saint Cyril and Saint Methodius,   pray for us.
Saint Charles Borromeo,   pray for us.
Saint Francis de Sales,   pray for us.
Saint Pius,   pray for us.

PRIESTS AND RELIGIOUS

Saint Anthony,   pray for us.
Saint Benedict,   pray for us.
Saint Bernard,   pray for us.
Saint Francis and Saint Dominic,   pray for us.
Saint Thomas Aquinas,   pray for us.
Saint Ignatius Loyola,   pray for us.
Saint Francis Xavier,   pray for us.
Saint Vincent de Paul,   pray for us.
Saint John Vianney,   pray for us.
Saint John Bosco,   pray for us.
Saint Catherine,   pray for us.
Saint Theresa,   pray for us.
Saint Rose,   pray for us.

LAITY

Saint Louis,	**pray for us.**
Saint Monica,	**pray for us.**
Saint Elizabeth,	**pray for us.**
All holy men and women,	**pray for us.**

III. INVOCATION OF CHRIST

A

Lord, be merciful,	**Lord, save your people.**
From all evil,	**Lord, save your people.**
From every sin,	**Lord, save your people.**
From the snares of the devil,	**Lord, save your people.**
From anger and hatred,	**Lord, save your people.**
From every evil intention,	**Lord, save your people.**
From everlasting death,	**Lord, save your people.**
By your coming as man,	**Lord, save your people.**
By your birth,	**Lord, save your people.**
By your baptism and fasting,	**Lord, save your people.**
By your sufferings and cross,	**Lord, save your people.**
By your death and burial,	**Lord, save your people.**
By your rising to new life,	**Lord, save your people.**
By your return in glory to the Father,	**Lord, save your people.**
By your gift of the Holy Spirit,	**Lord, save your people.**
By your coming again in glory,	**Lord, save your people.**

B

Christ, Son of the living God,	**have mercy on us.**
You came into this world,	**have mercy on us.**
You suffered for us on the cross,	**have mercy on us.**
You died to save us,	**have mercy on us.**
You lay in the tomb,	**have mercy on us.**
You rose from the dead,	**have mercy on us.**
You returned in glory to the Father,	**have mercy on us.**

You sent the Holy Spirit
  upon your Apostles,   have mercy on us.
You are seated at the right hand
  of the Father,   have mercy on us.
You will come again to judge the
  living and the dead,   have mercy on us.

IV. PRAYER FOR VARIOUS NEEDS

A Lord, be merciful to us,   Lord, hear our prayer.
   Give us true repentance,   Lord, hear our prayer.
   Strengthen us in your service,   Lord, hear our prayer.
   Reward with eternal life all
     who do good to us,   Lord, hear our prayer.
   Bless the fruits of the earth and
     of man's labor,   Lord, hear our prayer.

B Lord, show us your kindness,   Lord, hear our prayer.
   Raise our thoughts and desires
     to you,   Lord, hear our prayer.
   Save us from final damnation,   Lord, hear our prayer.
   Save our friends and all who
     have helped us,   Lord, hear our prayer.
   Grant eternal rest to all who
     have died in the faith,   Lord, hear our prayer.
   Spare us from disease, hunger,
     and war,   Lord, hear our prayer.
   Bring all peoples together in
     trust and peace,   Lord, hear our prayer.

C Always Used

> Guide and protect your
> holy Church, Lord, hear our prayer.
> Keep the pope and all the
> clergy in faithful service
> to your Church, Lord, hear our prayer.
> Bring all Christians together
> in unity, Lord, hear our prayer.
> Lead all men to the light
> of the Gospel, Lord, hear our prayer.

V. CONCLUSION

A Christ, hear us. Christ, hear us.
> Lord Jesus,
> hear our prayer. Lord Jesus, hear our prayer.

B Lamb of God, you take away
> the sins of the world: have mercy on us.
> Lamb of God, you take away
> the sins of the world: have mercy on us.
> Lamb of God, you take away
> the sins of the world: have mercy on us.

PRAYERS

A God of love, our strength and protection,
> hear the prayers of your Church.
> Grant that when we come to you in faith,
> our prayers may be answered
> through Christ our Lord.

> or:

B Lord God, you know our weakness.
   In your mercy
   grant that the example of your Saints
   may bring us back to love and serve you
   through Christ our Lord.